EMERGING AS YOUR BEST SELF

Molly Gicharu

Emerging As Your Best Self
Copyright © 2025 by Molly Gicharu

All rights reserved. No part of this publication may be reproduced, distributed, or transmitted in any form or by any means, including photocopying, recording or other electronic or mechanical methods, without the prior written permission of the author, except in the case of brief quotations embodied in reviews and certain other non-commercial uses permitted by copyright law.

Without in any way limiting the author's and publisher's exclusive rights under copyright, any use of this publication to "train" generative artificial intelligence (AI) technologies to generate text is expressly prohibited. The author reserves all rights to license uses of this work for generative AI training and development of machine learning language models.

Printed in the United States of America

Paperback ISBN: 978-1-965319-19-2

Purpose Publishing LLC.
13194 US Highway 301 South, Suite 417
Riverview, Florida 33578

www.PurposePublishing.com

FOREWORD

*I*f I were to encapsulate the essence of this foreword in a title, it would be "The Gift and Treasures of a Sister." Maureen, the author of this book, holds a sacred place in my heart as my baby sister, a bond that transcends time and will endure through the ages. However, it is impossible to speak of Maureen without acknowledging Jane, our other sister, with whom she shares an almost twin-like connection, separated by just 18 months. But until Jane shares her own story through her book, I will focus on Maureen's journey. Just as close to my is our only brother, Boniface, affectionately known as "Max." His courage and dedication to service in the US Marines profoundly influenced Maureen, inspiring her to follow in his footsteps and serve in the Army.

As the oldest sibling, I've had the privilege of watching Maureen grow and evolve, shaping her into the remarkable person she is today. Reading her book is a poignant reminder of her intrinsic value to the world and the profound treasury she represents to our family. For those fortunate enough to have cherished sisters or sisterhood friends, this narrative resonates with the joys and blessings these relationships bestow.

Belonging and Pride

Within the pages of my sister's book, you'll discover Maureen's profound sense of pride and belonging to her roots and community. Her journey is a testament to the importance of family support and the lasting impact of those who have guided her. Maureen exemplifies the essence of sisterhood—always having your back, especially during life's most challenging moments.

Endurance and Fortitude

Navigating different cultures across continents presents its own challenges—a theme illuminated in Maureen's book as she shares her experiences as an immigrant child adapting to new environments. Her resilience and fortitude shine through as she embraces change and rises to the occasion, exemplified by her remarkable journey in the military. Captain Maureen's ambition and determination inspire us all to dream big and persevere in the face of adversity.

Faith

One of the most inspiring aspects of Maureen's story is her unwavering faith in God. Her deep-rooted belief in divine providence and her active involvement in various Christian communities serve as a beacon of strength and hope throughout her narrative. As she shares stories of answered prayers and moments of divine intervention, Maureen's faith encourages us to trust God's plan, even amid uncertainty.

Adventures

One thing we share, my sister and I, is a zest for life and a love of adventure. It has led us to countless memorable experiences, from traveling to new destinations to trying new activities. One particular escapade stood out when we found ourselves on a desert safari in Abu Dhabi. A night under the stars turned into an unexpected solo adventure when the other tourists we had traveled with to the camp returned the same day. Despite moments of shock and disbelief, Maureen's courage and resilience prevailed, leaving us with cherished memories and valuable life lessons.

In Summary

Helen Keller once said, "Life is either a daring adventure or nothing at all," a sentiment that Maureen embodies. From traversing continents to embracing new opportunities in different states, she epitomizes the spirit of adventure and the courage to seize every moment. I hope that readers of this book will draw inspiration from Maureen's journey—navigating life with grace, embracing challenges, and sharing experiences with others to uplift and encourage them along the way.

Beatrice Gicharu

CONTENTS

Introduction ix
Chapter 1: Emerging As Your Best Self: Introduction . . . 1
Chapter 2: Growing Up 13
Chapter 3: The Journey Awaits 21
Chapter 4: Building New Foundations 27
Chapter 5: College Life-Undergrad 33
Chapter 6: Military Career - Part One 41
Chapter 7: College life-Graduate 51
Chapter 8: Military Career: Part Two 57
Chapter 9: Mentorship 65
Chapter 10: Friendship 71
Chapter 11: Self-Discovery 79
Chapter 12: Self-Belief 85
Chapter 13: Finances 91
Chapter 14: Breaking Stagnation 99
Chapter 15: Wholeness Journey 109
Chapter 16: Relationship 117

Chapter 17: My Entrepreneurship Journey 125

Chapter 18: The Power of Your Voice 139

Chapter 19: The Peak of My Life 149

Acknowledgment 159

About the Book 161

About the Author 163

INTRODUCTION

*I*n life, there are those who blaze trails for us—be it a relative, a historical luminary, or even a stranger. In the annals of American history, Rosa Parks, though departed, remains a towering figure. Her bold defiance, immortalized by a simple act of refusal, continues to ignite spirits across generations, especially among African American women, in the ongoing struggle for justice and parity.

In Kenya, the late President Jomo Kenyatta occupies a central position in the nation's fight for independence, spearheading the resistance against an oppressive regime. His boldness not only ignited the flames of liberation but also laid the groundwork for sustained endeavors toward justice and equality in the post-colonial landscape.

"Emerging as Your Best Self" chronicles the odyssey of my life, intertwined with the profound impact of those who have illuminated my path. Within its pages lie reflections on life's teachings, victories, and the audacity to chase one's aspirations. Among the constellation of influential figures are mentors, steadfast companions, paragons of virtue, women of unwavering faith, educators, nurturing parents, and, notably, my mother. This narrative will shine a spotlight on her unwavering presence, a steadfast beacon continually charting the course of my evolution.

Chapter 1

EMERGING AS YOUR BEST SELF: INTRODUCTION

My initial encounter with her began in the sanctuary of her womb, where I found solace, nurturing warmth, and the foundation for my growth. From the inception of my journey as an egg to the intricate stages of embryo development, the story unfolds, ultimately culminating in my arrival as a cherished baby girl—the final blessing to grace my parents' loving embrace. As the narrative unfolds, my intention is to vividly depict the myriad facets of this extraordinary woman—she is not only a devoted daughter, nurturing mother, devoted spouse, astute businesswoman, but also a beacon in our community, leading with grace and resilience.

Her essence, marked by unwavering faith, boundless generosity, relentless diligence, steadfast principles, resilient strength, cherished values, profound intellect, and timeless wisdom, has indelibly imprinted upon my soul. One poignant memory etched in my mind harkens back to a tumultuous juncture during my undergraduate nursing studies. Faced with daunting financial hurdles that threatened to derail my academic pursuit, I found solace in the unwavering support and belief in divine providence that emanated from my mother's unwavering spirit.

As the deadline for tuition payment loomed ominously, an unexpected phone call pierced through the tension, bringing with it a wave of unforeseen relief. Through the anonymous caller's revelation, a scholarship grant emerged seemingly out of thin air, generously covering the looming financial burden. This miraculous twist of fate flooded my heart with overwhelming gratitude, serving as a powerful reaffirmation of the significance of faith—a timeless lesson deeply ingrained within me by the unwavering guidance of my mother.

Amidst the trials of that turbulent period, the resounding echo of my mother's words reverberated within me: "Faith is believing in our answered prayers before witnessing the outcome." This poignant anecdote stands as but one thread in the rich tapestry of my journey, illuminating the profound impact of those who have cleared the path before me and the invaluable lessons gleaned along the transformative journey of self-discovery.

My admiration for my mother extends to her unwavering commitment to steadfast values. With grace and resilience, she exemplifies integrity, humility, and an unwavering respect for all, even when confronted with formidable personal trials.

Among the most trying episodes my mother has faced was the heartbreaking loss of her beloved family members. The first devastating blow came with the tragic passing of her sister, who succumbed to the anguish of her own inner turmoil. Recounting the harrowing details, my mother revealed that her sister, on the cusp of adulthood as a high school senior, harbored bright aspirations for her future, including a promising job opportunity in the bustling city of Nairobi, Kenya. Driven by sisterly love and support, my mother extended financial assistance to help her realize these dreams. However, the cruel betrayal of a man who had promised her sister employment led to coercion, deception, and ultimately, a grievous assault. Shattered by this horrific ordeal, her sister reached out to my mother, unveiling the agonizing truth of her plight.

Amidst the depths of her own sorrow, my mother steadfastly extended solace and guidance, urging her sister to seek assistance. Following a visit to the clinic, her sister returned home, seemingly safe. Yet, tragically, the next day bore the crushing news of her sister's untimely passing. Burdened by a profound sense of anguish and remorse, my mother grappled with the haunting notion of whether she could have done more to shield her beloved sister from harm. Despite her overwhelming grief, the community fondly remembered her sister as a woman of unwavering faith and resolute character, devoted wholeheartedly to the service of others.

Every day, my mother carries the enduring memory of her sister, often finding echoes of her presence in the strands of my long, black hair and the depth of my eyes. Amidst the ache of loss, my mother clings tightly to the precious memories they forged together as sisters and as a cherished family unit. In the face of such profound sorrow, her unwavering faith and steadfast trust in divine providence serve as steadfast pillars, offering solace and strength to navigate the tumultuous currents of grief.

The resilience of this remarkable woman faced yet another trial with the loss of her brother. I can still recall the somber day she returned home, bearing the heavy burden of devastating news. The sorrow etched in her eyes spoke volumes as she revealed the heartbreaking truth: the passing of her brother, my late uncle. His sudden demise at a bus station, possibly attributed to a heart attack, compounded the weight of grief upon my mother's already burdened heart.

My late uncle, a dedicated policeman, embodied kindness, cheerfulness, and a deep devotion to family. Despite residing far away in the Great Rift Valley of Kenya, my siblings and I eagerly anticipated our visits to him. Those road trips to the Great Rift Valley were not just journeys; they were adventures that exposed us to glimpses of wildlife and vistas of breathtaking scenery. Though the loss of my uncle left an irreplaceable void, it underscored the paramount importance of cherishing the moments shared with our loved ones. While the ache of his absence persists, my mother's gentle reminder to treasure our memories resonates deeply within me. Though we may feel he departed too soon, my mother finds solace in the belief that the Lord had ordained a different path for him.

The resilience of this extraordinary woman has been tested by numerous losses over the years, each one leaving an indelible imprint upon her heart. Among them was the passing of her father, who lived within the complexities of a polygamous marriage involving two wives. Her upbringing was enriched by the presence of both maternal and paternal grandparents, each contributing their own unique family dynamics to her formative years.

My maternal grandfather, blessed with ten children, including my mother, departed this world after I had the chance to know him. Conversely, my paternal grandfather, who embraced a family of four wives and over nineteen children, passed away at the age of ninety-five, a year prior to my birth. Although I never had the privilege of meeting him in person, his legacy echoed through the family lore, celebrating the inclusive environment he cultivated where every child was cherished as equal.

The adversities my mother has weathered throughout her lifetime stand as a testament to her unwavering resilience and deep-rooted faith. Her capacity to summon strength amidst sorrow not only speaks volumes about her extraordinary character but also underscores the profound values she imparted to her children.

Through my eldest sister, I uncovered the surprising revelation that my grandfather held the esteemed title of great-grandfather. Fortunately, I cultivated profound connections with both my maternal and paternal grandmothers—extraordinary women whose resilience and wisdom radiated brightly, despite their lack of formal education. In an era defined by traditional gender roles, where wives bore the mantle of household management and husbands assumed the role of primary breadwinners, my grandfather dutifully fulfilled his responsibilities.

As I write these words, my maternal grandmother, an extraordinary soul at the age of 108, continues to grace our lives with her presence. Regrettably, my paternal grandmother departed this world decades ago, having lived a remarkable life until the age of 104. Additionally, my maternal grandfather confronted a formidable battle with terminal prostate cancer, further underscoring the fragility and resilience of life's journey.

The memory of the day my mother received the devastating news about her father's declining health remains etched vividly in my mind. Despite his staunch aversion to hospital visits, the excruciating pain he endured necessitated urgent medical intervention. The diagnosis, delivered with solemn gravity, unveiled the grim reality: stage four prostate cancer with widespread metastasis. The doctor's prognosis was stark—a mere week left to live. At the time of her father's diagnosis, my mother was in the United States with her children, feeling the weight of physical separation keenly. Yet, amidst the anguish, she confided in us about a profound experience—a divine vision she received, foretelling the impending loss of a beloved family member.

Her ominous premonition sadly came to fruition when one of her brothers called, delivering the devastating news of our beloved grandfather's passing. The weight of grief bore heavily upon my mother, compounded by the remorse of not having the chance to bid her father a final farewell. Nevertheless, our family united in solidarity, extending unwavering support and heartfelt prayers during this profound moment of loss. Despite the exorbitant airfares amidst a peak travel season, we managed to secure plane tickets for my mother, elder sister, and myself to make the journey back to Kenya for the somber occasion of his burial.

As we navigated the preparations for the burial, the weight of financial obligations landed squarely on my mother's shoulders, shedding light on prevalent societal expectations and misunderstandings regarding immigrants living abroad. This ordeal starkly revealed the misconception that residing in a foreign land equated to boundless affluence. As a family, we grappled with unforeseen financial strains, exacerbated by the unwarranted assumptions of some relatives and acquaintances.

Despite the challenges, my grandfather's funeral proceeded as smoothly as possible. However, our grieving process was marred by an unexpected and terrifying event. One evening, while we were in our Nairobi home, armed gunmen accosted us, instilling fear for our lives. Unfortunately, the difficulties did not end there. Upon our return home, a shocking incident unfolded, turning what should have been a solemn homecoming into a nightmarish ordeal. Gunshots suddenly rang out on our roof as we hosted relatives and friends who couldn't attend the funeral. Panic gripped us as we realized the imminent danger we faced. Frightened, we sought cover, while my uncle hurriedly secured the front doors. Unable to breach our defenses, the assailants responded with more gunfire, leaving us traumatized by the harrowing experience.

Efforts to contact the local police proved fruitless, and upon their eventual arrival, their attention seemed disproportionately fixated on locating ammunition rather than providing immediate assistance. This disheartening experience shattered my sense of security within my parents' home and within Kenya itself. In response, our family promptly returned to the United States, where our second home offered a comforting sanctuary of safety and peace.

In the weeks that ensued, my mother, though projecting strength outwardly, bore the heavy burden of anguish deep within. She conveyed a profound sense of loss, mourning not only the passing of all her family members but particularly that of her father, with whom she shared an exceptionally tight bond.

We will forever hold dear the memory of my grandfather, a man of extraordinary qualities. His courage shone brightly as he valiantly served as militia and fought tirelessly for Kenya's independence. Through his poignant tales of survival and sacrifice during the war, he imparted invaluable lessons on the significance of family, faith, and the unwavering support of his beloved wife. His boundless generosity, demonstrated through both sharing fruits and imparting wisdom, etched enduring memories in the hearts of his grandchildren.

Though his passing left an indelible mark on my mother, as a united family, we strive to honor his legacy. We treasure his memory dearly, perpetuating his ethos of bravery, generosity, and the timeless importance of family values for generations to come.

I deeply admire my mother's selfless nature, a quality she embodies with unwavering dedication. The idea of selfless service, as defined by the Army as "prioritizing the welfare of others over your own," is not just a principle she embraces but one she lives by every day. Despite facing hardships in her upbringing where education was a luxury her family couldn't afford, my mother courageously entered the workforce at an early age. She set aside her own dreams to provide support for her siblings and aid her parents in their time of need.

She may have had limited educational opportunities herself, but she made sure to emphasize the importance of education to her children. She hoped they would achieve the dreams she couldn't. Her own dream of owning a business never faded; it continued to motivate her.

Starting as a secretary in a law firm, she encountered numerous challenges but never gave up. In a male-dominated auction industry, she obtained her auctioneer's license, showing remarkable courage. Her journey was filled with obstacles like evictions, facing familiar faces, and the uphill battle of being a woman in a male-centric field. However, she held firm in her belief that this was her calling, assigned by a higher power.

As her business expanded, she faced increasing challenges. Employee turnover and client poaching put her resilience to the test. However, she learned to overcome these obstacles, guiding her dream business to success and generating profits. Dieter F. Uchdorf's words ring true: "It's your reaction to adversity, not adversity itself, that determines how your life's story will develop." Her unyielding determination and resilience were the key to her success.

In addition to her business skills, my mother's remarkable qualities include her dedication to selfless service. Guided by her Catholic faith, she actively participates in the Catholic Women's Association, a group committed to community service. These women of faith engage in acts of kindness, like visiting the sick and providing essentials to the homeless. Spiritual practices such as adoration and worship are integral to their development. My mother's commitment to this organization has deeply influenced me, prompting me to join the Catholic Women of Faith as an adult.

In addition to her service, my mother's life has a sassy side. As a wife and mother, she delights in sharing stories of her courtship and marriage, revealing her charming and affectionate nature. Hailing from the Kikuyu tribe, her traditional wedding was steeped in rituals, highlighting the cultural practices of her heritage. Despite the societal norms of her time regarding marriage, her love story with my father shines brightly. The joyful ceremonies, rituals, and games of their traditional wedding highlight the cultural richness of the Kikuyu tribe.

Her parenting style, characterized by discipline and assertiveness, reflects a deep sense of responsibility. My parents imparted virtues of hard work, discipline, and perseverance to my siblings and me, nurturing us with strong moral values. While strict rules forbade sleepovers at friends' houses, the love notes and chocolates exchanged between my parents revealed a softer side, highlighting the tenderness within her.

In every facet of her life, my mother epitomizes selflessness, resilience, and courage. Her journey from modest beginnings to business triumph, alongside her dedication to service and family, portrays the image of an extraordinary woman. Her life narrative imparts invaluable lessons about overcoming challenges, serving others, and embracing one's courage, all of which contribute to the enduring legacy she is creating.

Reflecting on the chapters of my childhood, a story emerges marked by resilience, maternal love, and the fight against daunting childhood illnesses such as chickenpox, measles, and malaria.

Chickenpox, a highly contagious illness, brought about intense itching and blister-like rashes covering my entire body. Since there wasn't a chickenpox vaccine available during my early years, I was vulnerable to this viral attack. My mother recounted the difficulties she encountered while caring for me during my illness. Her vivid descriptions of the symptoms, the contagiousness of the disease, and its potential complications emphasized the importance of childhood vaccinations in preventing severe outcomes.

Despite being vaccinated against measles, I still contracted the disease as an infant, experiencing symptoms like high fever, a runny nose, and the telltale rash. My extraordinary mother shared the severity of my illness, worrying about my emaciated appearance and the challenges of keeping food down. The lack of compulsory vaccinations at that time heightened my susceptibility, an experience that spurred my mother to become a vocal advocate for childhood immunizations.

Malaria, a mosquito-borne illness prevalent in Africa, added to the series of health challenges I faced during childhood. Its symptoms, including fever, fatigue, and flu-like symptoms, presented a formidable foe. My mother's memories of my resilience during this battle highlighted the strength that emerged in the face of adversity.

Throughout these chapters of illness, my mother's unwavering care and prayers were instrumental in my recovery. Her dedication to nurturing me through these challenges, even in the absence of mandatory vaccinations, speaks volumes about the sacrifices mothers make for their children.

Reflecting on these childhood struggles, the importance of vaccinations resonates strongly with me. My individual experiences serve as a compelling endorsement for childhood immunizations, a sentiment I now share as a healthcare provider. It's a plea to parents to protect their children from preventable illnesses and a tribute to the sacrifices of mothers who navigate the uncertainties of childhood illnesses with boundless love and care.

The remarkable journey of this phenomenal woman, filled with courage, devotion, and sacrifices, continues to shape the narrative of my life. These trials have inspired me to advocate for childhood vaccinations, aiming to spare others from the battles I faced as a child. By acknowledging my mother's sacrifices, I strive to bridge the gap between the past and the present, where the legacy of resilience and the commitment to a brighter, healthier future stand as enduring guiding light.

REFLECTION

The innate longing for a better life, a dream cherished by the phenomenal woman, reflects the universal aspirations of every parent. Hindered by financial constraints that deprived her of a high school and college education, she channeled her aspirations through her children and grandchildren. An unexpected opportunity to move to the United States arose, prompting a profound sacrifice — the sale of all her properties to secure a brighter future for her descendants. This act epitomizes a mother's unwavering dedication to ensuring her children surpass the limits she faced, aiming for a life that transcends her own.

The genesis of this book lies in the echoes of that sacrifice and the bravery it took for her children to transition from the familiar to the unfamiliar in pursuit of a better life. The magnitude of the phenomenal woman's sacrifices is beyond easy comprehension; I, as one of her children, can only strive to bridge that gap by becoming my best self and making a positive impact on others.

The narrative draws inspiration from the selfless and courageous figures who, like Rosa Parks or President Jomo Kenyatta, paved the way for future generations. Their resilience and determination serve as guiding lights, illuminating the path toward a brighter future for all.

I take immense pride in my mother's journey, a testament to her resilience in achieving dreams despite formidable obstacles. My heart overflows with gratitude for her countless sacrifices, not only for her children but also for the service she rendered to others. The legacy of the phenomenal woman lives on in me, shaping the woman I am today. Her courage, adventurous spirit, prayers, perseverance, and grace have collectively shaped my identity.

This book serves as a vessel to share not only my life's journey but also the profound lessons learned from phenomenal women, mentors, role models, lifelong friends, and women of faith who have left an indelible mark. It is a journey towards inspiring others to break free from comfort zones, symbolized by the metaphorical hatching of an egg, urging each person to emerge as their best self.

As the words unfold on these pages, the goal is to maintain a simplicity that resonates with readers of all ages. The aim is to foster a genuine connection, enabling readers to find solace and inspiration in the sincerity of the narrative. May this book serve as a beacon of encouragement, inspiring all who engage with it to embark on their own journeys of self-discovery and emerge as the best version of themselves.

Chapter 2

GROWING UP

Throughout the chronicles of history, luminaries like the late Maya Angelou shine as beacons of inspiration. Their words and actions shape cultures and pave the way for countless others. My journey with Angelou's work began with her remarkable poem, "On the Pulse of Morning," delivered at President Clinton's inauguration. The sheer uniqueness and boldness of her artistry captivated me, prompting a deeper exploration of her story. Immersing myself in her acclaimed autobiography, *I Know Why the Caged Bird Sings*, I resonated deeply with her poignant declaration: "There is no greater agony than bearing an untold story inside you."

My journey unfolds against the backdrop of Nairobi, Kenya's bustling capital, nestled along Africa's eastern coast. Born and raised in this vibrant city, alongside my three older siblings—two sisters and a brother—I spent my formative years in Ngara, a lively residential area teeming with life and energy. I often reminisce with my elder sister and mother about our humble beginnings in our first home in Ngara, cherishing the memories that shaped our early years.

Ngara, with its myriad charms and challenges, presented a unique blend of opportunities and obstacles. The bustling open markets, brimming with fresh produce and essential commodities at affordable prices, served as a lifeline for many families. Vendors sold everything from clothes and furniture to a variety of foods, making Ngara a vibrant hub of activity. Commuting to the city was convenient, typically taking ten minutes or less, depending on traffic. The city's fast-paced life, with its whirlwind of activity and job opportunities, beckoned my parents, drawing them to Nairobi in pursuit of better prospects.

The allure of Ngara was not without its drawbacks, however. Pollution from nearby industrial facilities often tainted the air with unpleasant odors, a constant reminder of the environmental toll of urbanization. Safety concerns loomed large, particularly for children like my siblings and me. The crowded streets harbored potential risks, necessitating strict parental guidelines for our movements. We were always under the watchful eye of our elders, who enforced curfews and accompanied us to public spaces like the market, emphasizing the importance of vigilance and caution in our bustling surroundings.

We lived in Ngara for several years, enduring the trials and triumphs of cramped quarters and shared experiences. In our humble one-bedroom apartment, we forged unity amidst space constraints. It was a testament to the resilience of family bonds that we managed to thrive despite the crowded conditions. My elder sister and mother often reminisced about those days, reflecting on the simplicity of our existence and the camaraderie that sustained us through the challenges.

Life in our modest apartment presented obstacles, yet my parents navigated them with grace and determination. Despite the inherent difficulties, they ensured we lacked nothing essential, providing us with the necessities of life: food, water, and shelter. Our apartment, perched atop the building, offered a vantage point from which to view the world below, serving as a constant reminder of the journey we were undertaking together as a family.

The apartment offered a splendid view of the town and its amenities, with the convenience of running water and electricity. However, one drawback was the limited facilities: only two showers and one bathroom were shared among all the residents. This often led to conflicts, as everyone had to coordinate their bathing schedules. To avoid clashes, my parents would wake up early to shower before our neighbors, while my elder sister bathed us in the evenings. Despite these challenges, we felt enveloped in the unconditional love of our parents and each other, fostering a sense of unity and contentment that transcended the hardships.

My parents worked tirelessly to provide for us, holding multiple jobs to cover our housing and utility expenses. Meanwhile, my elder sister took on numerous responsibilities, from cooking and cleaning to caring for us and managing household chores. Despite the weight of these duties, she handled them with remarkable grace and maturity beyond her years, often sacrificing her own pursuits to support our family.

Reflecting on those formative years in Ngara, I am reminded of the resilience and determination that characterized our upbringing. Within the tapestry of these experiences, I find the roots of my inspiration, drawn from the indomitable spirit of individuals like Maya Angelou, whose words continue to resonate across time and space, guiding me on my journey of self-discovery and growth.

Our tenure in that apartment lasted until my parents could afford to purchase land in Mwiki, Kasarani, a residential area on the outskirts of Nairobi. The journey to building our own home was fraught with financial challenges, requiring my parents to work long hours to meet the expenses. After years of hard work and dedication, our family reached a significant milestone when we finished building our new house.

The transition to our new home in Mwiki was smooth, and I eagerly embraced the opportunity to start anew. The neighborhood was welcoming, and I relished making new friends and exploring my surroundings. Despite the longer commute to work, my parents prioritized our well-being while pursuing their aspirations.

My mother, fueled by a desire to become a business owner, embarked on a journey of self-improvement, attending training sessions and seeking guidance from mentors. Through perseverance and determination, she realized her dream of owning a printing company, a testament to her unwavering commitment to success.

Similarly, my father's journey exemplified the triumph of hard work and perseverance. Starting as an employee at various hotels, including the Hilton, he embarked on a path of upward mobility fueled by his unwavering dedication. Through countless hours of labor and a steadfast commitment to excellence, he ascended the ranks, eventually assuming the role of manager—a testament to his indomitable spirit and tenacity.

Yet, this journey was not without its sacrifices. My father's work demanded flexibility, often subjecting him to irregular shifts that disrupted our family routine. The unpredictability of his schedule, with shifts spanning day and night, required our family to adapt continuously. Despite these challenges, the sacrifices made by my parents laid a strong foundation for our family's future, instilling in us values of hard work, resilience, and unwavering support for one another.

Navigating through night and evening hours posed a challenge for us all. I vividly recall the unease I felt when my father worked the night shift; his disrupted sleep patterns reflected the delicate balance he maintained between professional obligations and his responsibilities at home. Despite the toll of lengthy commutes and fluctuating schedules, my father remained a beacon of strength and stability for our family. His unwavering commitment to providing for us, coupled with his boundless love and dedication, served as a wellspring of inspiration. Even as he traversed greater distances to fulfill his professional duties, his resolve never wavered, exemplifying the resilience and determination that defined his character.

Rooted in a small village upbringing in Thika, Kenya, my parents' journey to Nairobi to pursue better opportunities laid the foundation for our family's future. Their resilience, dedication, and unwavering commitment to our well-being inspire me as I navigate my own path forward.

As my siblings and I embarked on our educational journey, I was the youngest and last to start school. I remember feeling left out when my middle sister went to preschool, prompting my parents to enroll me early. Teachers noted my fondness for reading, though sports held less appeal for me. Forming cherished friendships while indulging in academic pursuits, I reveled in the camaraderie of school life.

Transitioning from day school to boarding school in fifth grade brought new challenges and opportunities. The structured environment of boarding school provided a comprehensive support system, fostering independence and personal growth. While separation from family was daunting, visiting days provided reassurance and connection.

Reflecting on my educational experiences, I am struck by the distinct yet complementary qualities of both day and boarding schools. Boarding schools offer a communal living arrangement that cultivates responsibility and independence, while day schools foster closer parent-child relationships and flexibility.

Both environments nurture creativity, academic growth, and invaluable life skills, preparing students for the challenges ahead.

The familial bond was the cornerstone of our upbringing, providing a nurturing environment for both academic and personal growth. These diverse experiences have sculpted me into the individual I am today, equipped with a versatile skill set and a broad perspective on education and life.

As my eldest sister ventured into high school, a new chapter unfolded for our family. Her academic prowess shone brightly as she excelled in her national exams, earning a coveted spot in one of the prestigious institutions. However, the distance of her chosen school from home posed logistical challenges, leading to the enlistment of a housekeeper to manage the household in her absence.

The absence of our eldest sister left a palpable void in our daily lives. Her presence had been a source of joy and inspiration, setting a high standard for us siblings to aspire to. Despite the physical distance, we remained steadfast in our support for her, cheering her on as she pursued her academic ambitions with determination and grace.

Meanwhile, my middle sister, brother, and I embarked on our educational journeys, transitioning from preschool and middle school to primary school. The daily routine of walking to and from school instilled a sense of independence and responsibility, marking the beginning of our gradual transition into adolescence.

As we matured, so too did our roles within the family dynamic. With each passing day, we assumed more significant responsibilities, both at home and in school, eagerly embracing the opportunity to contribute to the well-being of our family unit. Despite the challenges and uncertainties that lay ahead, we faced them with resilience and determination, buoyed by the unwavering support of our parents and the bond that bound us together as siblings.

Our new neighborhood was a breath of fresh air, quite literally. Gone were the noisy factories and polluted air. Instead, we enjoyed crisp, clean air and fertile soil. This pristine environment not only enriched our physical surroundings but also rejuvenated our spirits. It allowed us to reconnect with nature, cultivating our homegrown produce and livestock. As we adapted to our new surroundings, we rediscovered the joys of living in harmony with the land, savoring the simple pleasures of rural life amidst the bustling urban landscape.

REFLECTION

Life, with its blend of urban and rural experiences, presented its fair share of challenges and rewards. In the countryside, we cultivated fresh produce and tended to livestock, reaping the benefits of our labor through nourishing food. Conversely, the urban landscape, while offering job opportunities and convenience, was marred by environmental pollution, diminishing the land's fertility.

Reflecting on my childhood, I can't help but acknowledge the challenging yet formative experiences. Despite my reluctance towards chores, my parents laid a solid foundation in those early years, instilling in me the values of discipline, hard work, and perseverance. Attending both day and boarding schools further enriched my skill set, nurturing unique talents and aptitudes.

Above all, my upbringing taught me invaluable lessons in resilience and gratitude. It ingrained in me the importance of seizing opportunities, embracing challenges, and striving to become the best version of myself. Today, as an adult, I carry forward these principles, grounded in the understanding that life's journey is about continuous growth and self-improvement. My upbringing has shaped my perspective, reminding me to appreciate every blessing and never take anything for granted.

Chapter 3

THE JOURNEY AWAITS

As the sun dipped below the horizon on that picturesque Friday evening, the melody of birdsong filled the air, marking our return home from boarding school. My sister and I had grown accustomed to the routine of boarding school life since fifth grade, eagerly anticipating these reunions with our family and friends. The impending adventure of entering our junior year of high school added excitement to our anticipation.

However, this particular Friday held a surprise beyond our wildest expectations. As my parents returned home from work, they gathered my sister and me in the living room with news that would alter the course of our lives: in just one week, we would be leaving Kenya to visit our oldest sister in the United States.

The announcement was met with disbelief. Our older sister had been living in the USA for some years, navigating the challenges of single parenthood in a foreign land. The idea of joining her there seemed surreal to my teenage mind. Yet, as obedient children, my sister and I accepted our parents' decision without protest.

In the days leading up to our departure, amidst hurried farewells to friends and family, my sister and I found ourselves in a whirlwind of preparations. The week passed in a blur of shopping and packing until the moment of departure arrived.

Gathered tearfully at the airport, surrounded by loved ones bidding us farewell, my parents imparted words of wisdom that resonated deeply within me. "The world is tough," my mother said, her voice carrying the weight of experience. "You have to learn to be strong and adapt to any environment. Your parents won't always be there, and you must learn to survive." Her words, though daunting, were infused with a sense of love and guidance.

As the reality of our impending departure sank in, I couldn't help but feel a wave of apprehension wash over me. At just sixteen years old, with my middle sister barely eighteen, the prospect of caring for ourselves in a foreign land seemed daunting and overwhelming.

Yet, amidst the uncertainty, my mother's words of reassurance echoed in my mind, her unwavering faith in God's guidance as a source of comfort and strength. Raised in the Catholic faith and continuing to practice, I found solace in believing that God is an omnipresent presence who would accompany us on our journey, guiding our steps and illuminating our path.

As I embraced my parents, particularly my mother, tears welled in my eyes, a poignant reminder of the deep bond and love that bound us together as a family. The realization that I would soon be leaving the familiarity of our home, unprepared and uncertain of what lay ahead, filled me with a tumult of emotions.

With heavy hearts, my sister and I made our way to the airport, embarking on our first-ever airplane journey and venturing beyond the confines of our country. Every step felt surreal, every sight and sound unfamiliar as we navigated the bustling chaos of the airport.

Amidst the hustle and bustle of check-in, we meticulously ensured that we had all the necessary documents and that our luggage was securely packed. Despite the nerves and trepidation, there was a quiet resolve within us, a determination to face whatever challenges lay ahead with courage and resilience. As we boarded the plane, leaving behind the comfort of home and stepping into the unknown, I held onto the belief that with faith as our compass, we would find our way through the journey ahead.

Navigating the airport, everything felt unfamiliar and strange as my sister, and I embarked on our first-ever flight. The kindness of the air hostesses provided a reassuring presence as we settled into our seats, ready to embark on this new chapter of our lives.

Guided by my mother's instructions, the air hostesses took special care to assist us during transitions between terminals. As the aircraft prepared for takeoff, the cabin crew diligently followed safety protocols, ensuring each passenger was briefed on seat belt procedures, emergency protocols, and life jacket usage. With everything in order, the pilot signaled for departure, and I stole one last glance through the window at the familiar sights of Nairobi.

As the plane ascended, the reality of our departure sank in. With each passing minute, the distance between us and our homeland widened. The sensation of leaving behind everything familiar stirred a mix of emotions within me—nostalgia for the life I was leaving behind mingled with excitement and apprehension about the journey ahead.

As the aircraft soared higher into the clouds, I couldn't shake off a strange sensation in my stomach and eyes. Turning to my sister for reassurance, I found solace in her shared experience. Following her advice, I popped a piece of bubble gum into my mouth, finding comfort in the distraction it provided.

I marveled at the breathtaking view outside the window as the initial discomfort subsided. Once distant and unreachable, the clouds now enveloped us in their serene embrace. With each passing moment, the fear of the unknown gave way to a sense of wonder and excitement for the adventure ahead.

Yet, amidst the awe-inspiring scenery, a nagging sense of uncertainty lingered in the back of my mind. Thoughts of life in America, far removed from everything I had ever known, filled me with trepidation. In moments like these, my sister's steadfast resolve was a source of strength, reminding me of the bond that held us together.

Our journey, both literal and metaphorical, was beginning. With my sister by my side, I knew we would face challenges together, no matter the challenges. Our relationship, built on a foundation of love and laughter, would see us through the trials and triumphs that awaited us on the other side of the clouds.

REFLECTION

Looking back, I am reminded of immigrants' universal challenges in unfamiliar lands. While my journey may differ in specifics, the essence of overcoming obstacles and embracing new opportunities resonates deeply with the experiences of many.

Embarking on a journey to America required both courage and resilience. My sister and I had to muster the fortitude to venture into the unknown, trusting in our abilities and the wisdom of our parents. Our mother also displayed immense bravery, entrusting us with such responsibility at a tender age. It's a poignant reminder of Maya Angelou's words: "One isn't necessarily born with courage, but one is born with potential. Without courage, we cannot practice any other virtue with consistency. We can't be kind, true, merciful, generous, or honest." Our adventure was not just a test of our bravery but also of our faith, the bond of sisterhood, and our ability to navigate the unfamiliar.

Through the challenges, our sisterly bond strengthened, becoming as resilient as a tightly woven rope. Guided by faith, we safely reached the United States, our arrival a testament to the enduring power of perseverance and familial support.

Looking forward, I am motivated to empower others to unleash their potential and pursue their dreams with unyielding courage and determination. Our story is a beacon, demonstrating that with bravery and steadfastness, no obstacle is too formidable, and no aspiration is beyond reach.

Chapter 4

BUILDING NEW FOUNDATIONS

Arriving in the United States was a whirlwind of emotions. The first glimpse of the unfamiliar skyline filled me with wonder and trepidation. Everything seemed larger than life, from the sprawling highways to the towering skyscrapers. My sister and I were greeted at the airport by our eldest sister, whose face lit up with joy as she embraced us. In that moment, amidst the chaos of the bustling airport, I felt a glimmer of reassurance—a sense that, despite the challenges ahead, we had a piece of home with us.

Our journey from the airport to her apartment was filled with awe and curiosity. The endless rows of cars, neatly manicured lawns, and seemingly perfect suburban streets were a stark contrast to the vibrant, chaotic energy of Nairobi. The homes appeared uniform, with neatly trimmed hedges and American flags fluttering on porches. Yet, amidst the newness, I felt a deep longing for the familiarity of home—the bustling markets, the warm embrace of family, and the sounds of a city that never truly sleeps.

Setting into our new lives required significant adjustments. My sister's apartment was cozy but small, and we quickly realized the sacrifices she had made to provide for us. As we unpacked our suitcases, I couldn't help but feel a mix of gratitude and guilt. Her love and dedication to our family were evident in every corner of her home, from the carefully prepared meals to the thoughtful touches that made the space feel welcoming. I noticed little notes she had written on the refrigerator, encouraging us to stay focused and reminding us of our parents' love.

One of our first challenges was adapting to the American school system. Enrolling in high school mid-year felt like being thrown into the deep end. The cultural differences were stark, from the way classes were structured to the casual interactions between students and teachers. My sister and I often found ourselves leaning on each other for support, navigating the maze of new rules, expectations, and social norms. I recall the embarrassment of not understanding the school cafeteria system on our first day and the kind stranger who helped us navigate it.

The language barrier, though not insurmountable, was another hurdle. While we were proficient in English, the colloquialisms and accents often left us puzzled. Simple interactions, like ordering food or answering questions in class, sometimes felt daunting. Yet, with each passing day, we grew more confident, finding our footing in this unfamiliar world. I vividly remember the first time I raised my hand to answer a question in history class—a small but significant milestone in overcoming my fears.

Our weekends were spent exploring our new surroundings. From trips to local parks to grocery store outings, every experience was an adventure. I marveled at the variety of foods and products available, often comparing them to the markets of Nairobi. Despite the abundance, I found myself yearning for the simple, fresh produce of home, like mangoes and Sukuma wiki. These moments of nostalgia reminded me of the importance of holding onto our roots, even as we embraced new opportunities. My eldest sister often cooked traditional Kenyan dishes on weekends, filling the apartment with the comforting aromas of home.

Financial struggles were a constant reality. Our eldest sister worked tirelessly to make ends meet, juggling multiple jobs to support us. Her resilience and work ethic were nothing short of inspiring. She often reminded us of the sacrifices our parents had made to give us this opportunity and encouraged us to focus on our studies as a way of honoring their efforts. Watching her leave early in the morning and return late at night taught me the value of perseverance and the price of dreams.

The church became a sanctuary for us, a place where we found community and solace. Attending Sunday services provided a sense of continuity amidst the upheaval of our lives. The warmth and generosity of the congregation reminded us of the importance of faith and the strength it provides during times of uncertainty. I remember joining the youth choir and feeling an overwhelming sense of belonging as I sang hymns that echoed the prayers of my childhood.

Through it all, the bond between my sister and me grew stronger. We leaned on each other for comfort and encouragement, finding joy in the little things—shared laughter, late-night conversations, and the unwavering support that only siblings can provide. Together, we navigated the challenges of our new environment, drawing strength from our shared experiences and the unyielding love of our family. Our shared diary, where we wrote letters to our parents and documented our days, became a treasured source of connection and hope.

As the months turned into years, we began to build a new life for ourselves. The initial struggles gave way to moments of triumph—academic achievements, new friendships, and a growing sense of belonging. While the journey was far from easy, it taught us the value of resilience, adaptability, and the enduring power of love and faith. I remember the day I received my first academic award, a moment of pride and validation that I carried in my heart as a tribute to our collective efforts.

REFLECTION

Looking back, I am struck by the profound impact of those early years in America. My high school journey in both America and Kenya bestowed upon me a tapestry of diverse experiences and invaluable lessons, shaping me into the person I am today. In the United States, I seized the opportunity to immerse myself in American culture while proudly sharing the richness of my African heritage. Through simple yet profound gestures like offering Kenyan bracelets and accessories, and educating others about Africa, I endeavored to bridge cultural gaps and foster mutual understanding. They were a time of immense growth, shaped by challenges that tested our resolve and triumphs that reaffirmed our strength. The experience of starting anew in a foreign land taught me invaluable lessons about perseverance, gratitude, and the importance of family.

I am forever grateful to my eldest sister, whose sacrifices and unwavering support laid the foundation for our new lives. Her strength and determination continue to inspire me, reminding me of the incredible power of love and resilience. She taught me that success is not just about personal achievements but about lifting others as you climb.

These formative years instilled in me a deep appreciation for the opportunities I've been given and a commitment to paying it forward. As I move forward on my journey, I carry with me the lessons of those early days—a reminder that, no matter the challenges we face, we have the strength to overcome them and build a brighter future. These lessons fuel my desire to empower others, showing them that every obstacle is an opportunity to grow and thrive.

Chapter 5

COLLEGE LIFE

"It will not happen cutting corners, taking shortcuts, or looking for the easy way! There's only hard work, late nights, early mornings, practice, repetition, study, and discipline."

— Nimo Weheartit

Embarking on the journey of college life marked a significant transition for me. I pursued higher education after high school with a firm resolve, fully aware that achieving success would demand unwavering dedication, discipline, and perseverance. As a senior, I meticulously researched numerous colleges, both in and out of state, in search of the perfect fit for my aspirations. Ultimately, the University of Missouri Kansas City (UMKC) emerged as the ideal choice, aligning perfectly with my career goals in finance or healthcare. However, upon delving into the intricate details of tuition fees and financial aid options, I confronted a harsh reality—I lacked the financial resources to afford the tuition, and scholarships seemed out of reach.

Undeterred by this setback, I swiftly devised a new strategy: enrolling in a local community college as a more financially viable alternative. This decision compelled me to seek employment to sustain myself while concurrently pursuing my academic pursuits. With a coherent plan in mind, I embarked on securing employment. After diligent searching, I landed my first job in the healthcare field as a caregiver—a role that deeply resonated with my passion for serving others. Despite the uncertainty surrounding my career path, whether in finance or healthcare, I remained steadfast in my commitment to making a difference in people's lives.

As I navigated the complexities of college life, I was reminded of the words of Nimo Weheartit, emphasizing the importance of hard work, dedication, and discipline in achieving success. Despite the challenges and uncertainties that lay ahead, I was determined to persevere, knowing that each hurdle was an opportunity for growth and self-discovery. While my aptitude for mathematics and enjoyment of balance reconciliation hinted at a different career path, my experiences as a caregiver solidified my interest in healthcare. This realization sparked my interest in pursuing a career where I could leverage my skills and passion to contribute meaningfully to the well-being of individuals. My role as a caregiver presented an invaluable opportunity to gain firsthand insight into the field and clarify my career trajectory.

Working as a caregiver proved to be a profoundly enriching experience, providing me with a wealth of learning opportunities to refine my nursing skills and deepen my understanding of disease management and preventive care. Recognizing the importance of specialized senior care training, I took the initiative to enroll in a caregiver course. However, the journey to attend classes posed significant challenges, especially regarding transportation. Without a personal vehicle, I relied on the kindness of friends and public transportation to commute to the training center—a logistical puzzle that demanded creative solutions to navigate.

The acquisition of our first car, a modest blue Nissan Sentra purchased with my middle sister, alleviated our transportation woes. However, the initial excitement soon gave way to apprehension as the car began experiencing mechanical issues. Concerns about sudden breakdowns at traffic lights became a constant companion, tempered only by fervent prayers for smooth passage. Despite the car's quirks and occasional breakdowns, the acts of kindness from strangers and police officers who offered assistance during times of need served as a reassuring reminder of the inherent goodness in humanity. The vehicle, unreliable as it was, marked a significant milestone—a symbol of mobility and independence.

I persevered through the caregiver training program with determination, ultimately obtaining a nurse assistant (CNA) certification while diligently saving for college tuition fees. Each obstacle encountered served as a testament to the resilience and resourcefulness that would shape my path forward. The car dilemma persisted for nearly two years until we managed to save enough money to upgrade to a more reliable vehicle. Throughout this period, I often reflected on the stark differences in transportation systems between America and Kenya.

In Kenya, public transit primarily consists of buses, Nissans, or the ubiquitous Swahili matatus—vibrant minibusses adorned with colorful artwork and blaring music. Other modes of transportation include personal vehicles, trains, or even bicycles for shorter distances. Matatus are renowned for their lively atmosphere, characterized by pulsating music and a penchant for speeding through traffic. In contrast, America's public transit system is more structured, encompassing buses, trains, and private vehicles. Comparing these experiences highlighted the cultural and infrastructural nuances that shape daily life in both regions.

After completing my CNA certification, I dedicated myself to caregiving, honing skills in senior care, transfer techniques, and assisting patients with daily living activities. Eager to expand my knowledge, I enrolled in a certified medication technician course, completing rigorous training in clinical practices and theory. An opportunity for advancement arose within my workplace, leading to my transition into the role of a certified medication technician. Balancing work commitments with educational pursuits, I continued to pursue my passion for healthcare, eventually enrolling in nursing school. Starting at a community college for the first two years before transferring to a university, I navigated the complexities of financing my studies without the aid of scholarships.

The transition from high school to college proved demanding, requiring me to juggle multiple jobs while maintaining a full-time course load. Despite the challenges, I remained steadfast in my determination, fueling my efforts with cups of caramel chai latte to stay alert during lectures. College served as a crucible of adulthood, teaching me invaluable lessons in responsibility, time management, and fiscal prudence. Drawing on the wisdom imparted by my parents, who emphasized the importance of hard work and education, I forged ahead, propelled by a deep gratitude for the values instilled in me. My journey through college epitomized a period of profound growth and self-discovery, characterized by the resilience to overcome obstacles and the humility to learn from mistakes.

Continuing my college journey, I completed two and a half years at the community college, culminating in the attainment of my associate's degree in liberal arts. This milestone served as a steppingstone for my transition into nursing school. Despite the inevitable challenges encountered in nursing school, I persisted, ultimately obtaining my practical nursing diploma after the first year. Upon successfully passing my license certification exam, I was promoted to a charge nurse role at my previous job, effectively balancing my responsibilities while advancing my nursing career. However, amidst these successes, I encountered my first significant setback—a failed attempt at the national exam required to practice as a registered nurse.

The weight of this failure felt overwhelming, plunging me into a realm of uncertainty and self-doubt. Yet, in the depths of despair, I found solace in the unwavering support of my mother and sisters, whose encouragement served as a poignant reminder of the resilience ingrained within me. Summoning the strength to persevere, I sought guidance from a trusted professor and relied on the power of prayer to navigate the turmoil. With renewed determination and a comprehensive study plan, I approached the exam for a second time, ultimately achieving a passing score. Armed with my nursing license, I embraced the next chapter of my career with renewed vigor, assuming a role that demanded vital responsibility and unwavering dedication to the well-being of others.

As a registered nurse, I found fulfillment in making a tangible difference in patients' lives, navigating the complexities of leadership, delegation, and collaboration within interdisciplinary teams. Each day brought opportunities for growth as I forged lifelong friendships with colleagues and witnessed the transformative journey of patient recovery. Continuing to pursue my vision, I enrolled in a university and earned my Bachelor of Science in nursing. Feeling the need for change, I applied to a premier trauma hospital, embarking on a new chapter in my professional journey.

At this level one trauma hospital, I was immersed in a dynamic environment where every moment demanded focus, precision, and teamwork. Navigating emergency situations, from critical care patients to transplant services, honed my skills and instilled a profound respect for the resilience of the human spirit. I transitioned through roles—from bedside nurse to charge nurse to preceptor, and eventually, to transplant nurse. These experiences solidified my understanding of leadership and deepened my commitment to patient care.

Throughout my nursing journey, I pursued leadership training through John Maxwell's Mastermind program, which explored principles such as influence, process, and intuition. These insights transformed my perspective, equipping me to mentor graduate nurses and collaborate across disciplines. Leadership became both a professional skill and a personal calling.

My collegiate journey unfolded as a crucible where friendships blossomed, sculpting me into the person I am today. It was a period of immense growth, punctuated by a mosaic of experiences, bonds, setbacks, and newfound revelations. Witnessing patients triumph over seemingly insurmountable odds instilled within me a profound sense of fulfillment. The privilege of being entrusted with their well-being remains an enduring honor, fostering deep connections that transcend the confines of hospital walls. Upon reflection, I am profoundly grateful for the opportunities that have graced my path. Now, as I stand at the precipice of new horizons, I am compelled to pay forward the wisdom and experiences bestowed upon me, ensuring the flame of compassion and excellence continues to illuminate the journey for generations to come.

REFLECTION

The journey through college was a transformative experience—a testament to perseverance, resilience, and faith. From navigating academic hurdles to embracing new cultural experiences, every step enriched my perspective and strengthened my resolve. Each challenge I faced taught me invaluable lessons about adaptability, hard work, and self-belief.

Witnessing patients triumph over seemingly insurmountable odds—whether battling strokes, recovering from severe car accidents, combating sepsis, or undergoing organ transplants—instilled within me a profound sense of fulfillment. The privilege of being entrusted with their well-being remains an enduring honor, fostering deep connections that transcend the confines of hospital walls.

Moreover, these experiences not only cultivated lifelong friendships but also endowed me with invaluable skills and imbued me with a profound sense of humility. They also provided fertile ground for leadership opportunities, laying a sturdy groundwork for future roles and responsibilities.

Chapter 6

MILITARY CAREER - PART ONE

Embarking on my military journey marked a pivotal turning point in my life—a path characterized by profound moments of transformation and self-discovery. I vividly recall a crucial moment during my senior year in high school when a military recruiter visited our campus, sparking a dialogue that would ultimately shape my future.

As I absorbed the wealth of information provided by the recruiter, a sense of apprehension washed over me—an underlying fear of the unknown threatening to overshadow my aspirations. Yet, amidst the uncertainty, I found solace in the courage exemplified by my brother, who had already embarked on his military journey.

My brother had always been a source of inspiration and support—a beacon of bravery who navigated the unknown with unwavering resolve. His decision to join the United States Marine Corps stood as a testament to his steadfast commitment and dedication to serving his country. Observing his seamless transition from civilian life to military service, I couldn't help but swell with pride and admiration for his achievements.

Moreover, I realized that military service was not just a personal endeavor but also a legacy deeply embedded in our family's history. From my late grandfather, who fought for Kenya's independence as a militia member, to my late uncle and brother, our family had a longstanding tradition of service and sacrifice. This legacy inspired me to tread the path of service with honor and pride, echoing the commitment of generations before me to our respective nations.

A decade later, I found myself standing at the crossroads of a decision that would confront my deepest fears head-on. I had made the conscious choice to embrace faith over fear, electing to set aside my graduate-cohort program studies to embark on a journey of uncertainty and transformation.

As I approached the military processing center, a whirlwind of emotions enveloped me, ranging from fear and apprehension to a profound sense of duty and purpose. The prospect of delving into the unknown realm of military life stirred a mixture of trepidation and excitement within me. However, I was buoyed by the fervor of serving my nation honorably. Amidst the tumultuous swirl of emotions, a lingering tinge of sadness permeated my heart as I bid farewell to the familiar comforts of home, parting ways with cherished moments shared with family and friends. Yet, amidst the bittersweet farewells, I recognized that this journey was one of profound self-discovery and unwavering service—a path I resolved to embrace with wholehearted dedication.

Upon my arrival at the military processing center, I navigated through a series of stations, each step drawing me closer to the moment of truth. Amidst the bureaucratic formalities, I stood poised to take the final step—signing the contract and solemnly pledging to uphold the values and principles outlined in the Army-Reserve legislation. With a steadfast heart and resolute determination, I affixed my signature to the contract, symbolizing my unwavering commitment to serve and protect my country. In that profound moment, amidst the gravity of the oath-taking, I recognized that my life had undergone an irreversible transformation—a pivotal juncture that would indelibly shape the course of my future endeavors.

Embarking on this new chapter of my journey, I steeled myself for the trials ahead, fully aware that they would test me both mentally and physically. Before departing for military training, I conducted a thorough self-assessment, acknowledging that while I was mentally prepared for the challenges that lay ahead, my physical readiness required refinement. Armed with determination and resolve, I devised a rigorous exercise regimen to integrate into my daily routine. Setting modest goals, I committed to running at least two to three miles each day. Yet, despite my initial belief that the physical demands would be manageable, I soon realized that I had underestimated the true extent of the challenge before me.

In the weeks that followed, I persisted in my pursuit, steadily augmenting my physical strength and endurance. Drawing inspiration from my elder sister, who served as my unwavering companion and motivator, I found solace in her steadfast support and encouragement. Together, we navigated the trials and tribulations of the training regimen, propelling each other to surpass our boundaries and aspire for greatness.

Mentally, I embraced the Marine ethos that "pain is weakness leaving the body," employing it as a mantra to fortify my determination and persevere through moments of discomfort and exhaustion. With each passing week, tangible strides were made in both my physical capabilities and mental fortitude, reaffirming my conviction in the transformative influence of discipline and unwavering dedication.

As the day of my training departure approached, a sense of apprehension crept in, elevating my anxiety levels. To soothe these nerves, I turned to various relaxation techniques, such as deep breathing exercises and prayer, finding solace in moments of tranquility. Prayer became an essential aspect of my preparation, serving as a beacon of guidance amidst the uncertainties ahead. Initiating a novena—a nine-day petition prayer commonly practiced by Catholics—I dedicated myself to disciplined prayer, seeking strength, protection, and companionship throughout the training course.

With unyielding faith and determination, I embarked on this journey, fully aware that the forthcoming challenges would push my limits like never before. As the day of reckoning dawned, I embraced the path ahead with clarity and resolve, prepared to confront any obstacles head-on. As I stood amidst the airport's lively throngs, surrounded by the hum of travelers and the palpable excitement of the impending journey, poignant memories of heartfelt conversations with my family flooded my mind. My mother's words of concern resonated deeply as the departure day loomed closer.

Choosing to embark on this military path wasn't without its doubts and uncertainties. Yet, I clung steadfastly to my determination to confront whatever challenges lay ahead. Recalling a dream my mother shared—a vivid image of me in a field, one hand grasping a weapon while the other held a bag—I found a glimmer of solace in the notion that perhaps this path was predestined for me.

With the echoes of my family's support reverberating in my heart, I moved forward with a blend of resolve and apprehension, fully aware that the road ahead would be fraught with obstacles and trials. But bolstered by their unwavering love and encouragement, I embarked on this journey with purpose, ready to embrace whatever awaited me.

As I made my way through the bustling airport, each stride felt like a leap into the great unknown. Amidst the flurry of travelers and the buzz of departing flights, I seized a moment to indulge in a final meal before boarding. With my luggage checked and boarding pass secured, I headed toward the gate, poised to step into this next chapter of my life.

The journey to my training destination comprised two transits, each leg of the trip brimming with anticipation and introspection. As the aircraft soared through the vast expanse of sky, I found myself captivated by the world unfolding below, contemplating the path that lay ahead. With every passing moment, my resolve to fulfill my mission grew firmer.

Upon reaching the final transit point, the reality of the imminent training settled over me as I caught sight of my fellow trainees and felt the weight of responsibility descend upon my shoulders. Yet, amidst the uncertainty, a sense of camaraderie began to take root as I struck up a conversation with a fellow trainee, forging a bond that would bolster me through the trials to come.

As we congregated at the military office for check-in, the air crackled with palpable energy, a shared anticipation pulsating among us. With newfound companions by my side, I embraced the journey ahead with a sense of purpose and readiness.

Cloaked in confidentiality, the initial briefings hinted at the rigorous structure of the training. Divided into three distinct phases culminating in graduation, the program demanded unyielding dedication and resilience from every trainee. The first phase, in particular, proved to be a trial by fire, immersing us in relentless physical conditioning and daunting challenges. Despite the grueling demands, the training enforced a strict "free phone zone" policy, compelling us to prioritize our mission objectives and shun distractions. Stepping beyond my comfort zone, I embraced the challenge with unwavering resolve, pushing through setbacks with determination.

During a particularly grueling exercise, an ankle injury threatened to derail my progress. Yet, fueled by determination, I refused to let adversity hinder my journey. Employing the R.I.C.E. method—rest, ice, compression, and elevation—I nursed my injury back to health, resolute in my commitment to press on. With each passing week, I sensed myself growing physically and mentally fortified, my endurance forged by the challenges I confronted. Though the completion of the first phase seemed distant at times, I steadfastly rejected doubt, pushing myself beyond limits and emerging stronger for it.

Yet, the training dynamics took an unexpected turn when the drill sergeant thrust me into a leadership role—an unanticipated responsibility for which I felt ill-prepared added weight of leadership only amplified the demands on me, pushing me to the brink as I struggled to keep pace with the rigorous regimen.

As a leader, I was no longer accountable solely for myself but also for the trainees under my command. My days started earlier with leadership meetings, check-ins with drill sergeants, and ended late as I balanced my own training with new responsibilities. Determined to lead by example, I drew inspiration from astronaut Chris Hadfield's perspective on leadership:

"Ultimately, leadership is not about glorious crowning acts. It's about keeping your team focused on a goal and motivated to do their best to achieve it, especially when the stakes are high and the consequences really matter. It is about laying the groundwork for others' success, and then standing back and letting them shine."

Despite the mounting pressure, I persisted, navigating the trials of the second phase with resolute determination. Each passing week saw me becoming more adept at handling the challenges thrown my way, steadily inching closer to the ultimate goal of graduation.

As the second phase unfolded, I found my stride, ready to confront whatever obstacles lay in wait. Each week brought new trials, ensuring there was never a moment of respite. Despite grappling with the nuances of marksmanship, I persisted, refining my skills through tireless practice.

Yet, the training dynamics took an unexpected turn when the drill sergeant thrust me into a leadership role—an unanticipated responsibility for which I felt ill-prepared. The added weight of leadership only amplified the demands on me, pushing me to the brink as I struggled to keep pace with the rigorous regimen. Despite the mounting pressure, I persisted, navigating the trials of the second phase with resolute determination. Each passing week saw me becoming more adept at handling the challenges thrown my way, steadily inching closer to the ultimate goal of graduation.

As the second phase neared its conclusion, I prepared myself for the final stretch of the journey. To my surprise, the drill sergeants adopted a more relaxed approach, cultivating an atmosphere that made the final phase a surprisingly enjoyable experience. Throughout this phase, I witnessed the struggles of my fellow trainees, many of whom encountered obstacles threatening to derail their progress. Yet, bolstered by the camaraderie forged with my battle buddy, we remained steadfast in our determination to support each other until the very end.

After weeks of unwavering perseverance, the final phase drew to a close, signaling the beginning of graduation preparations. Reflecting with my battle buddy on our challenging journey, a profound sense of pride washed over us—we had endured the trials and emerged stronger for it.

Throughout the training, I cultivated enduring bonds with fellow trainees who, like me, had embarked on this transformative path. Guided by the drill sergeants, we underwent a profound metamorphosis, transitioning from ordinary individuals into seasoned warriors, poised to confront whatever obstacles lay ahead.

At last, the long-awaited graduation day arrived, marking the pinnacle of our rigorous training. With my father and sisters by my side, I stood tall as I received my accolades as an enlisted warrior. The pride shining in my father's smile spoke volumes, affirming that my dedication had not gone unnoticed. I felt deeply grateful for the unwavering support of my family, especially my sisters, who had been steadfast allies throughout every step of the journey.

Reflecting on my journey, the words of Friedrich Nietzsche resonated deeply: *"What doesn't kill you makes you stronger."* The challenges encountered during my military journey had indeed put my resolve to the test, yet they had also instilled in me a profound strength and resilience that would prove invaluable in the years ahead.

REFLECTION

What an extraordinary journey it has been! There are moments in life that demand celebration, and my military experience stands out as one of those pivotal moments. It was a time filled with profound pride and significance, especially the poignant moment when I had the privilege of saluting my earthly father—a memory brimming with accomplishment and pride.

Through the rigors of military training, a new sense of self emerged—a testament to the birth of resilience, discipline, honor, sacrifice, and the forging of lifelong friendships. The challenges encountered during training fortified my mental and physical fortitude, shaping my character and strengthening my resolve.

Reflecting on this journey, I am profoundly grateful for the warriors who have sacrificed and continue to dedicate their lives to serving their country. Their selflessness and unwavering commitment to a noble cause serve as an enduring source of inspiration, propelling me to pursue excellence in all endeavors. Additionally, I am deeply indebted to the steadfast support of my family and close friends, whose unwavering encouragement and love have sustained me through both triumphs and trials.

This journey has imparted invaluable lessons about resilience, camaraderie, and the profound significance of service. As I chart my course forward, I carry with me a profound gratitude for the experiences that have molded me and a renewed determination to honor the legacy of those who have paved the way before me.

Chapter 7

COLLEGE LIFE

Concluding the graduate cohort program marked the culmination of a series of noteworthy events in my life. Transitioning from the structured environment of military training to civilian life presented its challenges, but I was met with a warm reception upon returning home. Over time, I successfully acclimated to my new surroundings, buoyed by the joyous reunion with family and friends who eagerly awaited stories from my military experiences.

As anecdotes were shared, I highlighted the mental and physical challenges inherent in military training, reaffirming my commitment to maintaining the fitness levels attained during that time. Returning to work at the level one trauma hospital in the Midwest felt like slipping back into a familiar rhythm, with colleagues providing both comfort and camaraderie.

Simultaneously, I seized the opportunity to reignite my academic pursuits, meeting with my advisor to chart a course for completing the graduate cohort program. Together, we devised a comprehensive plan, delineating objectives and setting timelines to ensure a seamless reentry into the academic sphere.

Over the subsequent months, I adeptly balanced my responsibilities at the hospital with preparations for rejoining the graduate cohort program. As the final year of my academic journey loomed, I keenly felt the weight of expectation, but I embraced the challenge with determination and anticipation.

Balancing clinical hours and theoretical coursework presented a formidable challenge, but I was resolute in my determination to excel. Equipped with the resilience and discipline honed during my military training, I approached each day with a renewed sense of purpose. With every milestone achieved, I edged closer to the culmination of this chapter in my life, eagerly anticipating the opportunities and challenges that lay ahead.

Feeling the weight of juggling the demands of work and graduate studies, I made the decision to adjust my work schedule to a PRN position. This allowed me to allocate more time and energy to my academic pursuits. As both a warrior and a nurse, I understood the paramount importance of prioritizing my health amidst the demanding rigors of professional and academic commitments.

Empowered by the lessons gleaned from my personal journey, I embraced a holistic approach to well-being, recognizing the intricate balance between physical, mental, intellectual, and emotional health. Driven by a steadfast commitment to nurturing healthier habits, I embarked on a transformative path, prioritizing exercise, nutrition, hydration, and adequate rest.

Moreover, I sought to catalyze change beyond myself by fostering a culture of workplace wellness. Encouraging my colleagues to opt for the stairs over elevators, I aimed to seamlessly integrate physical activity into our daily routines. By doing so, I envisioned not only enhancing individual health but also fostering a supportive environment conducive to overall well-being.

Despite occasional setbacks in maintaining consistency with my exercise routine, I remained unwavering in my dedication to holistic well-being. I recognized that each small step forward contributed to my journey of self-improvement and resilience.

Balancing the demands of full-time school and work necessitated a disciplined approach, often characterized by early mornings, late nights, and limited rest. Within my workplace, a troubling pattern emerged—one that shed light on the disproportionate prevalence of diseases such as type 2 diabetes, hypertension, and kidney ailments in mortality rates.

This trend became particularly apparent during my tenure on the renal floor and in the float pool, where encounters with diabetic patients were all too frequent. The majority of my patients grappled with this condition, presenting a sobering picture of the health challenges faced by many in our community. The alarming statistics surrounding the trajectory of these diseases ignited a sense of urgency within me, compelling me to explore solutions that could disrupt this troubling narrative.

Drawing upon the invaluable lessons imparted by my undergraduate and graduate instructors, who ingrained in me and my peers the methodology of investigative inquiry, I embarked on a journey of research and problem-solving. My academic training provided me with the essential tools to systematically approach challenges—beginning with identifying the core of the issue and then devising and executing strategies for implementation. As a graduate student, I embraced the ethos of innovation, refining my skills through various research endeavors undertaken during my coursework.

Reflecting on my upbringing, I am reminded of my mother's unwavering emphasis on pursuing excellence in all endeavors. This foundational principle, instilled in me from childhood, manifested in my meticulous dedication to every project and assignment. This commitment to excellence was particularly evident in one of my most notable graduate projects—a collaborative effort with a project partner. Our shared dedication to achieving excellence propelled us forward, leading to significant outcomes.

Teaming up with my project partner, we embarked on an innovative endeavor aimed at combating the concerning rise of childhood obesity. Fueled by research findings highlighting the alarming rates of this health crisis, our joint mission was driven by a shared determination to enact tangible change within our community and beyond.

At the heart of our proposed solution lies a collaborative approach, recognizing the crucial role of primary care practices in identifying, educating, and implementing therapeutic interventions. Furthermore, we advocated for community-wide initiatives to promote physical fitness, advocating for the establishment of safe commuting routes to schools and the creation of affordable sports and fitness programs within local community centers.

Our collective efforts resulted in a comprehensive strategy that not only tackled the pressing issues surrounding childhood obesity but also paved the way for enduring, sustainable solutions. The recognition of our project's success, epitomized by the prestigious Bobbie Scholar Award for Evidence-based Practice in the primary care setting, served as a testament to the effectiveness of our collaborative teamwork, unwavering dedication, and commitment to upholding rigorous research standards.

As we look back on our achievements, we find inspiration in the potential for a healthier future for children across the United States. Our work, anchored in informed interventions, community engagement, and an enduring commitment to the well-being of the next generation, offers a beacon of hope for a brighter tomorrow.

REFLECTION

Working at a level one trauma hospital has been profoundly transformative, shaping both my identity as an individual and my journey as a registered nurse. Amidst the relentless pace of acute care, I gleaned invaluable lessons in teamwork, critical thinking, empathetic listening, disease management, and the promotion of health and wellness. Throughout my tenure, I was honored to receive esteemed accolades such as the Daisy Award for extraordinary nursing and MVP recognition for consecutive months, a testament to my unwavering dedication to patient care. Yet, the most meaningful recognition stemmed from the patients and colleagues whose lives I touched and the trust I earned.

Looking back, my time in acute care was punctuated by moments of profound fulfillment, particularly witnessing the recovery and healing of patients and their families. Moreover, the bonds forged during this period transcended professional boundaries, evolving into enduring friendships that continue to enrich both my personal and professional life.

Simultaneously, I embarked on completing my graduate program and transitioning into the role of a family nurse practitioner, a journey laden with its own unique challenges and rewards. As I navigate this new frontier, I am steadfast in my commitment to refining my communication skills, striving for proficiency, and delivering safe, high-quality patient care.

Chapter 8

MILITARY CAREER: PART TWO

Continuing the delicate balancing act between civilian life and military duties, I found solace and inspiration in the words of Roy T. Bennett: "It's only after you've stepped outside your comfort zone that you begin to change, grow, and transform." After two years of dedicated service as an enlisted member, I sensed a stirring within me—a yearning for change. I came to the realization that in order to evolve both personally and in my military career, I needed to bid farewell to my comfort zone and wholeheartedly embrace transformation.

The journey towards becoming an officer beckoned to me, spurred by a friend's referral to a recruiter. Thus commenced my pursuit of direct commission, a path I quickly realized was longer and more challenging than I initially anticipated, spanning over eighteen months. Despite the obstacles, I remained steadfast in my resolve, and finally, the day arrived when I proudly took the oath, surrounded by my immediate family who bore witness to the brief yet significant ceremony.

As an officer, I was met with immediate obligations, chief among them being the completion of mandatory training. This training encompassed three pivotal dimensions: direct commission training, as well as parts one and two of the introductory leadership course. With the transition to direct commission training, a new chapter in my military career began to unfold.

The commencement of training marked the initiation of a rigorous routine that spanned several weeks. Each day dawned with briefings, extending long into the night as we immersed ourselves in various exercises and drills meticulously crafted to hone our skills. From navigating challenging terrain to engaging in intense shooting drills, every task demanded our unwavering focus and dedication.

In my pursuit of growth and excellence, I embraced the delicate balance between civilian responsibilities and military commitments. Each day brought forth fresh challenges, yet it was by confronting these challenges head-on that I unearthed opportunities for personal growth and transformation. Venturing beyond my comfort zone, I uncovered the true essence of resilience and determination, virtues that would profoundly influence my journey.

One particular experience during the direct commission course remains etched vividly in my memory. It was an exercise in land navigation, tasking us with pinpointing specific locations within a designated area. Setting out before the break of dawn, my fellow trainees and I embarked on our journey towards the northwest of the mountain, greeted by the awe-inspiring spectacle of the sunrise painting the sky in vibrant hues of orange and pink. The panoramic vista of the mountains added to the splendor of the moment, prompting us to capture the scene in photographs before pressing onward with our mission.

Accompanied by my Battle Buddy, we adeptly navigated through the varied terrain, drawing upon our training to locate each point amidst the landscape. Despite the rugged terrain and unfamiliar surroundings posing significant challenges, we pressed on, drawing upon our knowledge of terrain features and navigation techniques. This experience proved deeply fulfilling, reaffirming our capabilities and fostering a strong sense of camaraderie among the trainees.

After weeks of rigorous training and countless obstacles overcome, we successfully completed all assigned tasks. With the direct commission course behind me, I returned home to embark on the next phase of my journey—the first part of the leadership course. Enrolling in the online portion of the course, I faced the additional challenge of balancing my full-time work commitments with the demands of training. Progressing through the modules at my own pace, I dedicated several months to mastering the course material, diligently completing each module and subsequent exams. Despite the time-consuming nature of the task, I remained resolute in my determination to succeed.

Finally, after months of unwavering dedication and perseverance, I successfully completed the online portion of the leadership course. This achievement was further validated during a week-long intensive course where I was awarded a certificate of completion—an affirmation of my steadfast commitment to personal and professional growth. Reflecting on the journey thus far, I was overwhelmed with a profound sense of pride and accomplishment, recognizing that each obstacle overcome had propelled me one step closer to the realization of my aspirations.

As my journey towards officer status progressed, the anticipated final stage of the leadership course approached—a field training session designed to assess our skills and readiness. Once again, I communicated with my manager and arranged for time off to fully immerse myself in the training.

Upon arrival, the training commenced with a thorough briefing and the distribution of schedules. This phase aimed to furnish us with essential leadership skills, emphasizing the significance of readiness and adaptability in executing our duties effectively. One aspect of military life that has always resonated with me is its inclusivity—where individuals are esteemed for their abilities and dedication rather than factors such as race, gender, or ethnicity. Interacting with a diverse group of trainees during this period underscored this fundamental principle, as we joined forces with a shared commitment to serve and protect our country.

Amidst the camaraderie forged during our training, the time-honored respect for the hierarchical structure within the military persisted—a tradition essential for instilling discipline and fostering cohesion among personnel.

Throughout the training, we encountered unforeseen challenges, including a severe weather forecast that disrupted our routines. Unprecedented snowfall blanketed the region for a week, leading to power outages and water shortages caused by frozen pipes. Despite these adversities, we remained resilient, adapting to the evolving circumstances with determination and flexibility.

As warriors, we embraced the ethos of adaptability, recognizing that challenges are an inherent aspect of our journey. Despite the disruptions caused by the inclement weather, we remained unwavering in our commitment to surmounting obstacles and fulfilling our mission. This experience served as a poignant testament to our collective resilience and determination, reaffirming our readiness to confront whatever challenges lay ahead.

Following the unexpected disruption caused by a week of adverse weather conditions, the trainers swiftly made necessary adjustments to our training schedule once conditions improved. With power and normalcy restored, albeit with some modifications, we resumed our training regimen with renewed focus and determination.

Field obstacles became our classroom, imparting invaluable lessons in survival and resilience. Each challenge provided an opportunity to refine our skills and showcase our readiness for future missions. Communication emerged as a pivotal element, essential for navigating the hazards posed by potential adversaries. Through effective communication, we mastered the art of risk mitigation and ensured the safety of our team.

Throughout the training, leadership roles were rotated among trainees, offering valuable opportunities to hone decision-making skills under pressure. Recognizing the weight of responsibility that accompanies leadership, we learned to think critically, heed guidance, and function as a cohesive unit. As leaders, we understood that our decisions could profoundly impact the mission's success and safety, underscoring the significance of sound judgment and teamwork.

The challenges of officer training pushed us to our limits, demanding discipline, resilience, and agility. Despite the trials, we persevered, growing more capable. Over time, I completed the training, forged lasting friendships, and gained invaluable insights for my career.

As training concluded, I returned home, reflecting on the journey. It tested my limits and prepared me for officer responsibilities. With newfound confidence, I looked to the future, ready for the next chapter with lessons from military training.

Stepping into my role as an officer, I realized the impact of mindset on leadership. Soon after, I transferred to a different unit, where fate intervened. What began as a simple task of covering for a fellow officer unexpectedly thrust me into a leadership position as platoon head. It was a responsibility I hadn't anticipated, yet one I was now tasked with embracing.

Stepping into this role, I was fortunate to have a mentor within our platoon—someone who refined my skills, provided guidance through the unknown, and, most importantly, believed in my abilities. His support was instrumental in my growth as a leader. A few years later, he himself stepped into the role of Commander—a position he was more than equipped for.

This experience taught me a valuable lesson: as you step into the unknown, there will always be people positioned to lift you up. Leadership is not a solitary journey—it is shaped by those who guide and believe in us.

With deep gratitude, I would like to thank you, Major-Patterson—for your unwavering mentorship and support.

Reflecting on my journey thus far, I realized that leadership had always been an inherent part of my path, whether in enlisted or officer training. With each new challenge, I had been called upon to step into leadership roles, gradually learning to embrace the responsibilities that came with them.

My perspective on leadership underwent a transformation as I settled into my new role. I understood that authentic leadership is rooted in service—serving others and shouldering the weight of responsibility on behalf of the team. As a platoon leader, it meant sacrificing personal comforts and dedicating myself to the welfare of my comrades. From attending meetings to ensuring that soldiers received crucial information, every action was driven by a commitment to serving those under my command.

Balancing my civilian leadership responsibilities with my newfound military role presented its challenges initially. However, through perseverance and determination, I began to navigate the delicate balance between the two, gradually mastering the art of juggling multiple responsibilities. I realized that leadership wasn't about seeking personal glory but rather about selflessly serving others and managing the uncertainties of the role.

With each obstacle overcome, I advanced in rank, eventually earning the promotion to captain—a testament to my leadership growth and development. Yet, even as I celebrated this achievement, I remained mindful of the journey ahead, knowing that the military would continue to test my limits in ways physical, mental, and emotional.

Uncertainty loomed as I stood at the threshold of the next chapter in my military career. Yet, with each passing season, I embraced the challenges that came my way, recognizing that each obstacle was an opportunity for growth and learning. My military journey was far from over, but with each step forward, I approached the unknown with courage and determination, prepared to rise to whatever challenges lay ahead.

REFLECTION

Embarking on a military journey is a profound shift, demanding both sacrifices and obligations. With each step, from enlisting to climbing the ranks, I am increasingly honored to serve my country and fulfill its missions. My recent promotion to captain marks not just a milestone but also a new level of leadership and responsibility.

This path isn't just about titles and duties; it's a constant evolution—a journey of resilience, faith, discipline, and grace. Despite its challenges, it continually surprises me, revealing depths of courage and commitment I never knew I possessed.

Amid the rigors of military life, I have learned the importance of balance, navigating both my service and civilian responsibilities with grace and determination. It is a journey marked by overcoming adversity and embracing the noble duty of serving my country, pushing myself beyond perceived limits.

None of this would have been possible without the unwavering support of my family and close friends, who have stood by me through thick and thin. To them, I owe an immeasurable debt of gratitude.

Reflecting on my military journey thus far, I am reminded of the virtues that sustain me and the profound impact of those who believe in me. It is a journey that continues to inspire, challenge, and shape me into the leader I aspire to be.

Chapter 9

MENTORSHIP

Mentorship, as defined by the Macmillan Dictionary, is the act of providing guidance and support to someone younger or less experienced over a period of time. In life's journey, the presence of mentors, coaches, and trusted friends is invaluable. I am fortunate to have encountered remarkable mentors and confidants who have played pivotal roles in my personal and professional growth.

According to Dr. KN Jacob, mentors serve as guides, sharing their valuable experiences and offering counsel to steer us away from potential pitfalls. They illuminate the path forward, helping us navigate the complexities of life. Beyond guidance, mentors act as connectors, aiding us in forging valuable relationships and discovering our life's purpose. They are trusted advisors who nurture and challenge us to reach our fullest potential.

In my pursuit of purpose and fulfillment, I sought mentors who could help me unlock my gifts and explore untapped opportunities. Whether in education or various life ventures, I have been privileged to cross paths with mentors whose wisdom and support have been priceless assets on my journey. Their presence has boosted my confidence and kept me accountable, ensuring I remain focused and driven toward my goals.

MY MENTORS

My Mother

Foremost among my mentors is my mother, whose unwavering guidance has profoundly shaped the person I am today. Her grace, prayerfulness, exemplary character, and unconditional love have been constant sources of strength and inspiration.

Miss Beatrice

Another influential mentor on my journey is Miss Beatrice. As a self-made entrepreneur, sister, mother, confidant, and editor, she has continually poured into me, challenging me to reach greater heights. Her dedication, hard work, and resilience—especially as a single mother—have been a powerful example. From excelling academically in Kenya to supporting our family's transition to the United States, she has demonstrated the value of perseverance and setting ambitious goals.

Miss Beatrice's journey as an entrepreneur in the real estate industry is particularly inspiring. Despite numerous challenges, including single parenthood and furthering her education, she achieved remarkable success. Her story is a testament to resilience, determination, and the power of intentional living.

Dr. Masters

In the captivating tapestry of my mentorship journey, Dr. Masters stands out as a beacon of wisdom and grace. With a doctorate in nursing and a career spanning acute care and academia, she has modeled excellence in every facet of her professional life. Her humility and compassion set her apart, creating an atmosphere ripe for growth and learning.

Dr. Masters' influence extends beyond her achievements. She supported me during my graduate studies, guiding me through academic challenges and personal growth. When I faced obstacles securing clinical hours, she stepped in as my preceptor, a selfless act that profoundly impacted my journey. Her mentorship was instrumental in my development as a healthcare professional, instilling confidence and practical skills.

Dr. Lorna

My final mentor, Dr. Lorna, is not only a trusted guide but also a dear friend. Her illustrious career as an internal medicine physician and her unwavering dedication to her community exemplify balance and grace.

Through her mentorship, Dr. Lorna has pushed me out of my comfort zone, encouraging me to develop critical skills such as public speaking and networking. Her guidance has been instrumental in fostering valuable connections and providing insights that have shaped my path.

The Impact of Mentorship

In each of these mentors, I have found guidance, wisdom, and unwavering support. Their influence has shaped my journey, inspiring me to strive for excellence and pursue personal and professional growth. The lessons they have imparted—resilience, determination, and the importance of continuous learning—serve as a foundation for my aspirations.

Mentorship is more than guidance; it is a transformative relationship that empowers individuals to realize their potential. I am profoundly grateful for the mentors in my life, and I aspire to emulate their example by uplifting others as they have uplifted me.

REFLECTION

Gratitude fills my heart as I reflect on the invaluable guidance and wisdom bestowed upon me by my mentors throughout my journey. Their influence, whether direct or indirect, has left an indelible mark on the person I am today. Among the myriads of lessons they've shared, one principal shines brightly: the art of balance.

Under their tutelage, I have learned to navigate the delicate dance of balancing priorities, delegating tasks, and periodically reassessing strategies—a skill set essential not only for personal success but also for traversing life's intricate tapestry. Moreover, my mentors have emboldened me to continually challenge myself, urging me to wholeheartedly embrace growth beyond the confines of comfort.

Their mentorship transcends mere professional advancement; it encompasses the essence of personal evolution. By encouraging me to broaden my horizons through voracious reading, active participation in seminars, and engaging in thought-provoking discourse, they have empowered me to transcend limitations and unlock my fullest potential.

At the core of their guidance lies the importance of networking—not as a transactional pursuit, but as a genuine commitment to building authentic connections. As one mentor succinctly put it, networking is as simple as initiating a conversation rooted in authenticity and a shared purpose.

I extend heartfelt gratitude to my mentors, whose wisdom has illuminated my path. I stand as the woman I am today because of your guidance and support. In the spirit of Maya

Angelou's timeless wisdom, I am compelled to pay it forward: *"When you learn, teach; when you receive, give."*

Grit, tenacity, and hard work remain the bedrock of their teachings, serving as constant reminders that success is not a gift, but a reward earned through disciplined effort. They have instilled in me the understanding that discipline is the linchpin upon which achievement hinges—a muscle to be exercised and fortified with unwavering resolve.

Chapter 10

FRIENDSHIP

Friendship, I've discovered, is a state characterized by enduring affection, esteem, intimacy, and trust between individuals. Its profound impact on our lives cannot be overstated. However, just as not all seeds yield a harvest, not all connections blossom into genuine friendships.

In my journey to grasp the nuances of friendship, I've gleaned insights from various sources. One particularly enlightening perspective comes from a luminary figure in life, leadership, and spirituality—Bishop T.D. Jakes. His profound understanding of friendship sheds light on its multifaceted nature.

Bishop Jakes delineates three fundamental aspects of friendships: confidants, constituents, and comrades. Confidants, he explains, are rare and invaluable. These friends love you unconditionally, enriching your life rather than draining it. They stand as beacons of unwavering support, offering truths and standing by your side through thick and thin.

Building upon Bishop T.D. Jakes' insightful categorization of friendships, we delve into the second type: constituents. Unlike confidants, constituents are marked by fluctuating seasons. At times, discerning them from confidants may prove challenging due to certain similarities. However, constituents possess the potential to disappoint or lead astray, highlighting the transient nature of these relationships.

Lastly, Bishop Jakes introduces comrades—a friendship forged for a specific season or mission. Comrades are allies united by a shared purpose or goal, yet their loyalty extends solely to the mission at hand. Once the task is accomplished, comrades may part ways, their connection dissipating with the fulfillment of their collective objective.

As I delved deeper into the intricacies of friendship, I confronted the unsettling truth that not all connections are meant to accompany us on our journey to the next chapter of life. This realization stirred unease as I endeavored to carry all my friendships through every season.

Armed with newfound insights into the diverse facets of friendship, I embarked on a journey of introspection, reevaluating my relationships through Bishop T.D. Jakes' categorization. To my astonishment, I discovered that my friendships spanned across all three categories delineated by Bishop Jakes.

At the heart of my social sphere, I cherish my confidants—individuals who have earned a place in my inner circle through years of shared experiences and mutual respect. These friendships, built on shared values and authenticity, have weathered life's storms alongside me. Despite the ebb and flow of daily communication, the bond with my confidants remains unbreakable. We understand and embrace each other's need for space, respecting each other's boundaries without apology. In the rare moments when we do connect, the rapport is instantaneous, as if no time has passed. In confidant friendships, reciprocity reigns supreme—a testament to the adage that to have a great friend, one must first be a great friend.

Continuing my exploration of friendships, I delve into the category of constituents. Upon reflection, I realized that some of my connections fell into this category, initially resembling confidants. However, upon deeper examination, I understood why these friendships failed to thrive. Naively, I had shared my deepest aspirations and dreams, seeking support, only to be disappointed. This realization brought about emotional turmoil, but with time and newfound wisdom, I now possess the tools to guard my heart more effectively.

According to Bishop T.D. Jakes, the final dimension of friendship is that of comrades. These friendships are distinct and easily discernible. Throughout my journey, comrades have appeared in various seasons of my life—during work, academic pursuits, or collaborative projects. However, I've learned to recognize that these friendships, while significant in their own right, are often transient, bound by the specific mission or season they were forged in. Though initially perplexed by the eventual fading of these connections, I now understand that such friendships are inherently seasonal.

In addition to the delineated categories of friendships, another type holds significant sway in my life—the women of faith. While their classification may elude conventional categorization, their impact is undeniable. These women, whom I've encountered through various avenues such as community gatherings, church congregations, Bible study fellowships, and retreats, have left an indelible mark on my journey.

Having been raised in the Catholic faith, I've come to perceive spirituality not as a matter of religious affiliation but rather as a deeply personal relationship with the Divine. The women of faith I've had the privilege to know come from diverse religious backgrounds, yet they share a common commitment to seeking the Divine and embodying their faith in tangible ways.

I deeply admire the unwavering dedication, selfless service, and steadfast support exhibited by these women of faith.

Whether through community outreach initiatives, caring for the less fortunate, or simply offering a shoulder to lean on, they exemplify the essence of faith in action. Moreover, their resilience in the face of adversity serves as a beacon of hope and inspiration. I've witnessed their triumphs over personal trials and tribulations, marveling at their ability to navigate life's challenges with unwavering faith and grace.

My introduction to the community of faithful women was profoundly shaped by the influence of my family, particularly my mother, whose exemplary life served as a beacon of faith. Growing up under her guidance, I was immersed in the culture of belonging and service within our religious community. Through her, I became acquainted with a group of devout women in Kansas City and joined a vibrant women's Bible study fellowship.

Within this community, I cultivated deep and meaningful relationships with fellow women of faith. Together, we shared experiences, worshiped collectively, and supported one another through life's challenges. These interactions not only tested my faith but also strengthened it, akin to the way muscles grow stronger through rigorous exercise.

Despite our modest numbers, the women of faith in Kansas City exhibit a remarkable spirit, reminiscent of David facing Goliath. Our gatherings are marked by fellowship and a commitment to the Catholic motto—a guiding principle of our shared faith.

As an active member of this community, I have been deeply involved in various initiatives, including organizing youth groups and participating in the Catholic Women's Association (CWA). As a member of the CWA, we are dedicated to nurturing our spiritual growth through communal worship and service. Following the principles of the CWA, we engage in acts of mercy, reach out to our community, participate in adoration, and provide support to the sick. Our gatherings are characterized by joyous celebration and communal prayer, fostering a profound sense of unity and solidarity among members.

Reflecting on my journey as a young woman, I am profoundly grateful for the trailblazing women of faith who have illuminated my path. Their steadfast examples have reignited a deep intimacy with the Lord—a connection never truly lost but nurtured and reaffirmed through their guidance.

Upon relocating to Atlanta, Georgia, I found solace in continuing my involvement with the faith community and Bible study fellowship. Additionally, serving in the children's ministry has brought immense joy and fulfillment, allowing me to impart faith lessons to the next generation.

I extend my deepest gratitude to all the women of faith who have left an indelible mark on my life. Through shared challenges and triumphs, I've gleaned invaluable lessons in service, generosity, humility, and the transformative power of prayer. They have enriched my journey and paved the way for countless others to walk in the light of faith.

Reflecting on my life journey, I've come to understand the profound impact friendships have had in shaping my experiences and decisions. While some friendships have added immense value to my life, others have caused a sense of disconnection. This serves as a reminder of the importance of anchoring oneself amidst the ever-changing nature of relationships.

By categorizing friendships, I've gained clarity and insight, enabling me to better protect my heart. I've realized that friendships can be seasonal, each serving specific purposes or missions. Understanding the rarity of true confidants, I've learned to cherish and nurture those relationships while establishing boundaries to safeguard myself.

Appreciating the diversity of friendship seasons, I'm rediscovering how to discern the true nature of these connections. Not all friendships are built for deep trust, yet each has contributed to my growth and personal development. As Vladimir Lenin once said, "Show me who your friends are, and I will tell you who you are." Regardless of their category, I am deeply grateful to all my friends for enriching my life and helping me become the best version of myself.

REFLECTION

Self-discovery has been integral to my personal growth journey, requiring me to equip myself with specific tools and virtues to navigate the path ahead. Among these virtues, mindset, discipline, consistency, tolerance, and patience have emerged as crucial pillars anchoring my journey.

Patience, in particular, resonates deeply with me, akin to the growth process of a bamboo tree. Just as a bamboo tree takes several years to sprout and grow, self-discovery requires nurturing, time, and perseverance. Initially, progress may feel elusive, much like the invisible growth of a bamboo tree in its early years. However, with dedication and commitment, gradual changes manifest, eventually leading to visible growth and transformation.

I've come to understand that patience is not merely a virtue but a daily practice—a continuous effort to persevere even when progress feels slow or non-existent. It involves embracing the journey with resilience and determination, persisting through setbacks and challenges.

As I continue to cultivate patience, I am reminded that self-discovery is a journey of ongoing growth and learning. Each small step forward brings me closer to realizing my full potential. Just as I persist in my pursuit of personal growth, I encourage you to do the same—to embrace patience as a guiding principle on your journey of self-discovery.

Chapter 11

SELF-DISCOVERY

Embarking on the journey of self-discovery is like delving into the mysteries of one's existence—an expedition of revelation and growth. It's a deeply personal quest marked by introspection, reassessment, and transformation. In this chapter, I extend an invitation to join me on this intimate journey as I unveil the habits for success that have sculpted my life.

Along my path of self-discovery, I've gathered invaluable lessons that have fueled my personal evolution and equipped me to uplift and motivate others. Through sharing these insights, my intention is to illuminate the path toward a more enriching and purposeful existence.

At the heart of this exploration lies the pivotal role of habits—the fundamental drivers of success. Within these pages, I'll intimately examine the habits that have served as the bedrock of my journey, offering tangible insights and actionable wisdom to fuel your pursuit of self-improvement.

Furthermore, I'll illuminate the profound impact of immersing oneself in certain literary works on the journey of self-discovery. From timeless classics to contemporary gems, literature has acted as a beacon, providing invaluable lessons and diverse perspectives that have deepened my understanding of both me and the world.

Embark with me on this odyssey of self-discovery as we navigate the intricate pathways of habits and insights that possess the transformative power to elevate lives and propel us toward our utmost potential.

From my perspective, success transcends the mere achievement of goals or aspirations; it embodies the essence of effecting positive change and solving problems. This transformative shift in perception was sparked by my encounter with Steve Harvey's enlightening tome, *Act Like a Success, Think Like a Success*, which offered a profound reimagining of the very concept of success.

Harvey contends that true success isn't just about achieving personal milestones but about being a trailblazer—someone who innovates and tackles real-world challenges with creativity and determination. At the heart of this philosophy lies the belief that one's past doesn't have to define one's future; instead, success involves honoring one's roots while forging ahead with clear intention and unwavering purpose.

This newfound perspective on success shattered my previous narrow view, which solely equated success with academic accomplishments. I came to understand that genuine success extends far beyond individual achievements; it's deeply rooted in acts of service. Whether it's serving others, the community, family, strangers, or humanity as a whole, true success is intricately linked to acts of kindness and generosity.

Empowered by this transformative insight, I underwent a profound shift in mindset, embracing a more comprehensive definition of success—one centered on both service and innovation.

In my relentless pursuit of unraveling the secrets of success, I delved deep into the realm of habits, fervently seeking out the practices that pave the way to greatness. Through meticulous research and voracious reading, I uncovered a wealth of self-discovery habits that have propelled me toward unlocking my fullest potential.

Within the expansive realm of success, I've distilled a handful of transformative habits that continuously propel me toward new horizons. Among these practices is the ritual of rising at dawn—a habit synonymous with the pursuit of excellence.

The early morning hours possess a remarkable potency, providing a sacred sanctuary for introspection, creativity, and productivity. In this tranquil window, untouched by the clamor of the day, miracles unfold, and breakthroughs take shape. Inspired by Robin Sharma's seminal masterpiece, *The 5 AM Club*, I've gained a profound appreciation for the impact of seizing the morning and taking full ownership of the day.

Sharma eloquently expounds on the notion of the morning victory, underscoring the significance of commencing each day with purpose and intentionality. Through his teachings, I've learned to harness the transformative potential of the early hours, laying the groundwork for a day brimming with productivity, growth, and fulfillment.

Within the pages of his book, Sharma elaborates on three fundamental concepts that underpin the morning ritual: the significance of early rising, the benefits of physical exercise, and the cultivation of mindfulness through reflection and meditation. By embracing these principles, I've unlocked new levels of productivity and fulfillment, paving the way for a life brimming with purpose and passion.

In Sharma's framework, the initial phase of this transformative journey is aptly termed the "disruption phase." Spanning twenty-two days, this phase demands unwavering dedication to rising before sunrise—an endeavor aimed at unlocking one's true potential.

I vividly recall the early days of adopting this new habit—it was undeniably challenging. There were mornings when the allure of sleep seemed insurmountable, and maintaining consistency felt like an uphill battle. Yet, in those moments of struggle, I realized that sheer willpower alone wouldn't propel me to the next level of achievement. What I truly needed was a steadfast commitment to discipline and consistency.

Fueled by an unyielding desire to ascend to new heights, I consciously prioritized my dedication to personal growth. This involved establishing boundaries and routines meticulously crafted to support my journey toward self-discovery. One such boundary entailed refraining from checking my phone and emails in the morning—a deliberate choice aimed at safeguarding the sanctity of my early hours for tapping into my full potential.

As I embraced this newfound discipline, the fruits of my labor began to materialize. The early morning hours became sacred, dedicated to creativity and self-expression. In these quiet moments before dawn, I immersed myself in crafting my first book—a testament to the transformative power of my morning ritual.

Each day brought a renewed sense of momentum and purpose. Creativity flowed effortlessly as I transitioned into the next phase of my journey, marked by sustained momentum and growth.

According to Sharma's progression, the phase following disruption is termed integration. As Sharma eloquently puts it, *"All change is hard at first, messy in the middle, and so gorgeous at the end."* This phase signifies the culmination of transformation—a time when new habits seamlessly integrate into daily life.

I recognized the necessity for continued support and dedication to navigate this phase successfully. Mastery of any habit demands persistence and unwavering consistency, typically spanning twenty-two days. Drawing upon Sharma's wisdom, I formulated a strategy to maintain momentum and surmount obstacles.

One of Sharma's pivotal principles on habit formation proved invaluable during this period: the significance of delving deeply to propel oneself to the next level, even amidst the allure of quitting. Armed with this insight, I remained resolute in adhering to my schedule, undeterred by internal resistance or doubt.

Through steadfast commitment and perseverance, I gradually transitioned into the final phase of habit formation—the integration phase. According to Sharma, this phase typically extends for at least sixty-six days, embedding the newly acquired habit deeply into daily rituals.

REFLECTION

Self-discovery has been integral to my personal growth journey, requiring me to equip myself with specific tools and virtues to navigate the path ahead. Among these virtues, mindset, discipline, consistency, tolerance, and patience have emerged as crucial pillars anchoring my journey.

Patience, in particular, resonates deeply with me, akin to the growth process of a bamboo tree. Just as a bamboo tree takes several years to sprout and grow, self-discovery also requires nurturing, time, and perseverance. Initially, progress may feel elusive, much like the invisible growth of a bamboo tree in its early years. However, with dedication and commitment, gradual changes manifest, eventually leading to visible growth and transformation.

I've come to understand that patience is not merely a virtue but a daily practice—a continuous effort to persevere even when progress feels slow or non-existent. It involves embracing the journey with resilience and determination, persisting through setbacks and challenges.

As I continue to cultivate patience, I am reminded that self-discovery is a journey of ongoing growth and learning. Each small step forward brings me closer to realizing my full potential. Just as I persist in my pursuit of personal growth, I encourage you to do the same—to embrace patience as a guiding principle on your journey of self-discovery.

Chapter 12

SELF-BELIEF

WHAT IS SELF-BELIEF? According to the Berkeley Well-Being Institute, self-belief is "having confidence in your abilities." It involves trusting oneself to pursue a specific goal or dream, knowing that efforts will result in desired outcomes. Self-belief is nurtured through experiences of self-worth, self-confidence, self-trust, self-respect, and surrounding environmental mastery (Berkeley Well-Being Institute, 2023).

The concept of self-belief was profoundly enriched during my attendance at a virtual Growth Day platform conference led by Brendon Burchard. Brendon Burchard is renowned as a motivational speaker, author, and the founder of the Growth Day platform, among other accomplishments. At this conference, Jamie Kern Lima, a notable American entrepreneur, media personality, and co-founder of IT Cosmetics, shared her insights on self-belief. She described it as "the decision to believe in one's dream, knowing it is possible." It involves understanding oneself internally and making a deliberate choice to trust in one's vision or dream. Jamie Kern Lima's powerful story of overcoming challenges serves as a poignant reminder that all things are achievable for those who believe. I highly recommend her book, *Believe It: How to Go from Underestimated to Unstoppable*.

With newfound insight into self-belief, I took time to reflect on my understanding of overcoming self-limitations. In my younger years, I struggled with self-belief, a struggle rooted in a specific memory from elementary school. I remember attending class with eagerness, only to have a teacher declare that I would never amount to anything significant. Those hurtful words echoed in my mind persistently. However, that moment became a catalyst for me to prove them wrong.

Moreover, I resolved not only to become the best version of myself but also to give back to the same elementary school. Two decades later, I achieved more than I had imagined on my journey of growth. I anonymously sponsored a child and founded a nonprofit organization aimed at empowering children and feeding homeless youth. Through these actions, I realized that my purpose transcended merely proving my teacher wrong; it was about fulfilling a deeper calling.

Another pivotal moment in my entrepreneurial journey involved confronting self-limiting beliefs. Despite having vision and drive, I faced challenges rooted in fear of failure, procrastination, and reluctance to leave my comfort zone. Attending a business conference, I encountered a speaker who introduced a profound exercise on self-belief. She began by dissecting the word "believe," highlighting that within it lies the word "lie," prompting a fresh perspective on its depth.

The speaker then distributed wooden boards, instructing us to write our goals on one side and our self-limiting beliefs on the other. This physical representation empowered action. With the support of an accountability partner, I committed to breaking through these barriers. Focusing my thoughts and believing in my ability to overcome, I approached the challenge with determination.

When I successfully broke the board, a surge of pride and joy swept over me, met with cheers and celebration from fellow attendees. This moment marked a significant shift in my understanding that self-limiting beliefs stem from our thoughts, past experiences, and life encounters. It reinforced that liberation from these beliefs requires proactive action and belief in oneself.

During my college years, I faced a significant challenge in overcoming my lack of self-confidence, particularly during public speaking and interpersonal communication classes. These courses required regular speeches and presentations to large audiences, something that initially intimidated me due to my self-limiting beliefs.

Seeking guidance, I turned to my mother for advice. She encouraged me to practice in front of a mirror and start each session with self-affirmation. Her metaphorical advice, likening me to a lion in courage, inspired me to adopt a confident posture and demeanor while rehearsing. Initially feeling awkward, I persisted, repeating the exercises until I began to notice a profound shift. Gradually, my inner confidence grew, reflecting in my outward performance.

With each speech and presentation, my anxiety lessened, replaced by a growing assurance in my abilities. Through consistent practice and my mother's wisdom, I learned to transcend my self-doubt and develop a newfound self-confidence that extended beyond the classroom, impacting various aspects of my life.

Another pivotal moment in overcoming my self-limiting beliefs was when I embarked on writing my first book. I had always harbored a dream of becoming an author, but procrastination and avoidance held me back. Despite encouragement from a supportive mentor who repeatedly asked about my progress, I found myself making excuses and deflecting the topic.

As the years passed, the desire to fulfill my dream grew stronger until, one year, I made a crucial decision: to set a firm deadline. Establishing this deadline forced me to take action and maintain consistency in my writing process. I soon discovered that writing not only progressed but also became a therapeutic endeavor for me.

Setting that deadline was transformative, but the real breakthrough came through the act of writing itself. I realized the importance of surrounding myself with supportive individuals who held me accountable and refused to accept my excuses.

Through this experience, I learned firsthand the value of setting clear goals and surrounding myself with people who motivate and challenge me to achieve them.

A pivotal factor in my journey was developing a deep belief in myself and my writing. I vividly remember listening to Les Brown's podcast, where he eloquently described the cemetery as one of the wealthiest places on earth, filled with unrealized innovations, unwritten books, and dreams left unfulfilled. This insight inspired me to tap into my full potential while alive. I rejected the grip of procrastination and embraced a proactive mindset, determined to take decisive action and trust in my abilities.

As I continue to grow, so does my self-belief, a cornerstone of artistic expression. I've learned that others cannot believe in you unless you first believe in yourself. Entrepreneur Robert Herjavec once said, "It is impossible to get ahead in life without taking risks," a truth I embraced wholeheartedly in writing my first book. It required unwavering faith in my craft and the courage to seize opportunities. The journey demanded early mornings, consistent effort, and personal sacrifice, all anchored in a steadfast belief in myself.

Even now, I find strength in affirmations—powerful tools for reinforcing, inspiring, and motivating oneself. Louise Hay's teachings on affirmations resonate deeply with me, and I highly recommend her approach for anyone seeking to bolster their self-belief. Louise Hay educated me on how affirmations aid in rewiring the brain, particularly during times of weakness or low spirits.

REFLECTION

What a profound journey self-belief has been for me! It's about liberation, overcoming obstacles, and personal transformation. Self-belief is an inner voyage that radiates outwardly. It demands vulnerability, authenticity, courage, and decisive action. In my heart, I made the decision to pursue my purpose through writing, believing steadfastly in myself and my artistic vision. Self-belief feels like taking a leap of faith in oneself!

I encourage others with these words: *"Believe in yourself! Have faith in your abilities! You cannot be successful or happy without a humble but reasonable confidence in your own powers."* — Norman Vincent Peale.

To anyone grappling with self-doubt, I share my story in the hope that it uplifts you and inspires you to start believing in yourself more than ever before. Every step on this journey is worth it.

Chapter 13

FINANCES

David Bach once said, "Before you can start setting financial goals, you must determine where you stand financially." Reflecting on my own financial journey began with introspection into my knowledge, background, and habits. Growing up, I witnessed my parents grappling with financial challenges. Money was a topic rarely discussed at home—no conversations about budgeting or financial planning. I realized early on that achieving financial stability required excelling in education and securing a well-paying job.

In this chapter, I will share my journey through financial failures, the lessons I've learned, and how I navigated toward financial stability.

My first real encounter with money came when I secured my first job. While attending college, I juggled two jobs to help pay for tuition and cover other expenses. Despite my efforts, I soon realized that my income was insufficient to cover all my school fees. Additionally, I did not qualify for any grants or scholarships, leaving me in a tough financial spot.

My next step was to apply for credit cards, which marked the beginning of my financial troubles. Without a solid understanding of credit card management, I made several mistakes.

After covering my tuition fees, I found myself spending money on unnecessary items like clothes, shoes, and accessories.

Moreover, I relied on credit cards for emergencies. A significant incident was when my late grandfather was diagnosed with terminal prostate cancer. I used my credit card to pay for my flight to Kenya and other travel expenses. With limited finances, credit cards became my lifeline, but this reliance led to a precarious financial situation.

Another financial mistake I made was taking cash advances. At the time, I was unaware that cash advances carried higher interest rates compared to regular credit card charges. I vividly remember falling seriously ill during one semester and needing to visit the hospital. Unfortunately, I didn't have health insurance and was unaware of the possibility of requesting financial assistance for hospital bills. I paid my medical expenses using credit card cash advances, not fully understanding the consequences.

Utilizing cash advances led to a situation where I had to repay significantly more than I had borrowed. My final mistake was missing several credit card payments, which severely impacted my credit score, plummeting it from excellent to poor.

As a diligent student, I learned from my financial mistakes and embarked on a journey toward better fiscal management and credit repair. It began with an honest assessment of my financial situation and setting clear goals for where I wanted to be. My primary objective was to achieve financial freedom and eliminate money-related stress.

I turned to Suze Orman, a renowned financial guru, for guidance. Her mantra, "People first, then money, then things," resonated with me. She emphasized the importance of prioritizing essentials and living within one's means to achieve financial stability. Inspired by her advice, I set out to change my financial habits, starting with learning to prioritize my expenses.

One of the first habits I tackled was impulse buying. Before making any purchase, I would ask myself if the item was a want or a need. This practice helped me avoid unnecessary expenditures. Another principle Orman emphasizes is the necessity of saving for emergencies. She advises having at least eight months' worth of emergency savings.

With this in mind, I set up a savings account and started saving small amounts, gradually increasing my contributions each month. This intentionality in saving was crucial for building a financial safety net.

Through disciplined habits and breaking old patterns, I continued working on my fiscal management skills. Prioritizing needs over wants and saving diligently were key steps in my journey toward financial stability.

My elder sister and I took a course by financial expert Dave Ramsey, which focused on the seven aspects of achieving financial freedom. This class was transformative, providing me with practical steps and a clear roadmap for managing my finances.

The first step was to establish an emergency fund with at least one thousand dollars in savings. Next, we learned to pay off debts using the snowball method, excluding the mortgage. The third principle was to save three to six months' worth of expenses in a fully funded emergency fund.

The fourth step involved investing fifteen percent of household income into retirement funds. The fifth principle emphasized saving for children's college education. The sixth principle encouraged paying off the home mortgage early. Finally, the seventh principle was to build wealth and give generously.

This course was an eye-opener, providing me with the guidance I needed to take control of my finances. I adopted a more authentic approach, taking inventory of my financial situation and holding myself accountable. I meticulously listed all my student loans, credit card debts, monthly expenses, and income in a notebook. This comprehensive overview helped me create a clear plan to tackle my financial goals systematically.

The next step was to implement the lessons I had learned. I had already started saving for emergencies as recommended by financial guru Suze Orman. I incorporated savings for both regular expenses and unexpected emergencies. Initially, it was challenging, but I improved over time.

I took inventory of my student loans and debts, reaching out to the financial institution managing my student loan to explore my options. Unfortunately, I did not qualify for any financial assistance. Nevertheless, I was determined to pay off my student loans and credit cards.

To ensure timely credit card payments, I set up monthly auto-debit payments through my bank. This system prevented me from missing payments and incurring additional fees.

Next, I focused on paying off my student loan. While it was challenging initially, I started to see progress each month, which kept me motivated. Through these steps, I began to gain control over my finances and work toward financial stability.

In 2020, a new act was introduced that suspended interest on student loans for six to eight months due to the COVID-19 pandemic. I seized this opportunity to make considerable progress on paying off my student loan. By cutting my expenses and paying down some of my credit card debts, I made substantial strides in my financial journey.

By the end of 2020, I had paid off all my student loans, settled all my hospital bills, cleared most of my credit card balances, and started building my emergency fund. Achieving these milestones required discipline, self-sacrifice, and intentionality—principles I continue to incorporate into my financial journey.

Reflecting on my financial missteps and the knowledge I've gained; I am eager to share the lessons I've learned and how I turned things around.

The first lesson was understanding the proper use of credit cards. I educated myself on the basics of credit, including the three major credit bureaus: Equifax, TransUnion, and Experian. Building and maintaining a good credit score involves several key practices:

1. **Timely Payments:** Always making monthly payments on time and never missing any expenses.
2. **Credit Diversification:** Diversifying my credit portfolio.
3. **Credit Utilization:** Using only up to thirty percent of my credit card limits.
4. **Avoiding Cash Advances:** Steering clear of cash advances, which had previously jeopardized my financial stability.

These are just a few of the fundamental habits I practice on my financial journey. By following the advice of financial gurus and committing to these practices, I have improved my credit scores and continue to live authentically within my means.

To further rebuild my finances and enhance my knowledge, I turned to books and podcasts focused on financial management. Two books that greatly influenced me were *Smart Women Finish First* by David Bach and *Choosing to Prosper* by Bola

Sokunbi. Bola Sokunbi also runs an online financial platform called Clever Girl Finance, which aims to empower women with financial knowledge.

In addition to reading books, I found value in listening to financial podcasts and watching YouTube channels dedicated to personal finance. These resources provided diverse perspectives and practical advice, helping me make informed decisions and stay motivated on my financial journey. Seeking expert guidance and continually educating myself have been crucial in achieving better fiscal management and stability.

On my financial journey, I learned the importance of money affirmations and donations. Affirmations play a crucial role in rewiring one's brain and building self-esteem, and they can be applied to any area of life, including finance. My favorite money affirmations are by Louise Hay. One that particularly resonated with me is, *"I move from poverty to prosperity thinking, and my finances reflect this change."* This affirmation helped me shift my mindset from scarcity to abundance.

I also embraced the practice of giving, a lesson instilled in me by my mother. She often said, *"It is always greater to be a giver than a receiver,"* emphasizing the importance of contributing to our church tithe. Inspired by her words, I began donating ten percent of my gross income, not just my net income. This habit led to increased charitable giving and support for various organizations.

One of my proudest achievements was starting and launching Beacon of Light, a non-profit organization dedicated to feeding children in Kenya and empowering both boys and girls. I discovered that the more I gave, the more I received in return, both personally and financially. This practice of sowing seeds and reaping the harvest has become a cornerstone of my financial journey.

Incorporating these principles of affirmations and giving has helped me build a solid foundation for financial freedom. As I continue on this path, I remain committed to these practices, continually reinforcing my financial resilience and generosity.

REFLECTION

In reflecting on my financial journey, I've identified various habits that set successful people apart. Here are some key practices:

1. **Valuing Time and Planning Wisely**: Successful individuals understand the importance of time management. They meticulously plan their days, setting clear priorities and goals.
2. **Diversifying Investments**: They recognize the importance of diversifying their investments to optimize returns and minimize risks.
3. **Multiple Income Streams**: Successful people often have multiple sources of income, reducing their dependence on a single revenue stream and enhancing financial stability.
4. **Financial Discipline**: Building and maintaining financial discipline is crucial. This includes budgeting, saving, and making informed spending decisions.
5. **Seeking Financial Guidance**: They are not afraid to seek advice from financial experts to make better-informed decisions and stay on track with their financial goals.
6. **Generosity**: Many successful people are generous givers. They understand the value of contributing to causes

they believe in and the positive impact it has on their communities and themselves.

By incorporating these habits, I hope my financial journey serves as a testament to the attainability of economic freedom. With determination, discipline, and the right practices, anyone can achieve financial success.

Chapter 14

BREAKING STAGNATION

"To change your world, one has to change your mind first. It all begins with your mind," T.D. Jakes once said. I embraced this wisdom and decided it was time to break the stagnation in my life. Through introspection, I identified the areas needing change and wrote down my vision and goals. Using a cardboard poster with various highlights, I clearly outlined these goals and pinned them to my bedroom wall, inspired by the Book of Habakkuk's advice to write your vision clearly.

With my vision set, it was time to get to work. Progress was uneven, with some months bringing significant strides and others marked by stagnation. Determined not to fall back into old patterns, I sought guidance from a life coach and a mentor, understanding that I couldn't navigate these changes alone.

I invested in the Growth Day platform, an online community founded by Brendon Burchard, a motivational speaker and author. Growth Day connects leaders, speakers, and learners with the shared goal of personal and professional development. My elder sister had recommended this community, and after two years, I had witnessed tremendous growth in various aspects of my life.

To accelerate this progress, I hired a life coach to help me unravel my patterns and guide me to new heights. Initially unfamiliar with the work of life coaches, I quickly learned their value in providing the insight and accountability needed for personal transformation. Through the guidance of my life coach and the supportive environment of the Growth Day community, I began to see significant improvements and felt more empowered to achieve my goals.

I knew I was open and flexible to new perspectives. The program I joined lasted about eleven weeks, with each session running one to two hours. The sessions focused on twelve elements: focal points, courage, psychology, purpose, energy levels, and more. Here, I will share a few of these elements.

The first element was dissecting the focal point. The session began with introspection on various areas of one's life. The life coach helped identify the current focus and aided in breaking any stagnation. This included recognizing everyday habits, whether productive or not. At that time, my main focus areas were completing my first book and improving my health.

We examined seven key areas that could hinder one's focal points: friendship, love, mission, finances, hobbies, spirituality, and health/well-being. The first assignment was to rate these seven areas on a scale of 0-10 to assess my current standing. Following this, I identified triggers that affected my focal points. Together with my life coach, we implemented new habits and skills to help me reach a level 10 in each area, aiming to live a charged and fulfilling life.

The next session focused on **clarity**. In the clarity session, the process began by selecting three words that would propel me to the next level. Each word was chosen to serve a specific purpose: one to remind me of who or what I want to be, another for how I want to interact with others, and the final one to signify what will make me successful.

The first word I chose was **positivity**. I consider myself a positive person, and I aim to continue radiating positive energy and remaining open to new perspectives. This helps me stay focused on my goals and maintain a constructive outlook.

The second word I chose was **hope**. Hope is about seeing great things even before they happen, believing in endeavors and people despite obstacles. It's a driving force that keeps me motivated and optimistic.

The final word I chose was **courage**. Courage is essential for taking risks and pushing boundaries. Without it, one cannot reach the next level. I am committed to taking risks to achieve my aspirations.

The session concluded with a reflection on one's "why" in life. Understanding my "why" is crucial as it drives me each day. It represents a purpose greater than me and is worth fighting for. This exercise was powerful and thought-provoking, providing me with profound insights into my motivations and goals.

I continue to implement my three chosen words—positivity, hope, and courage—to reach the next level in my journey. They serve as daily reminders of my commitment to personal growth and success.

The next session focused on **energy levels**, which encompass four key areas: mental stamina, brain fog, feelings of aliveness, and resilience. Energy levels play an essential role in one's life. The session began with an assessment of my energy levels in these four areas.

The first focus was on brain fog. Upon introspection, I noticed that my brain fog fluctuates in the morning—sometimes I feel creatively charged, while at other times, not as much. The life coach then guided me on how to manage and maximize my mental clarity. Strategies to stimulate the brain include reading books, meditating, and adopting other beneficial habits. These practices can help enhance mental clarity and overall awareness.

The second area of focus was **mental stamina**. The session began by rating one's stamina level on a scale of 0-10. Evaluating mental stamina throughout the day is important as it encompasses exercise, nutrition, and rest.

Exercise plays a crucial role in mental stamina and includes physical fitness routines. Individuals are encouraged to develop an exercise regimen for at least five out of seven days a week. This routine should include cardio workouts and aerobics for at least fifty minutes. Such exercises help optimize lung function and overall energy levels.

Optimal nutrition is another key aspect of mental stamina. It involves increasing hydration and adopting healthy eating patterns. This includes eliminating white starches, carbohydrates, and sugar from the diet and instead focusing on vegetables, whole grains, and fruits to boost mental stamina. Additionally, nutrition can be supplemented with multivitamins, fish oil, magnesium, and other essential vitamins. Incorporating these supplements helps reduce the risk of disorders such as diabetes, obesity, and dementia.

Lastly, **rest** is essential for maintaining elevated levels of mental stamina. Adequate rest is vital, with the recommendation for optimal sleep being at least seven or eight hours per night. Developing consistent sleeping habits and patterns allows individuals to optimize their rest and recovery.

The last two elements of energy levels are **feeling aliveness** and **resilience**.

The process of assessing aliveness begins with evaluating your current state. Recommended habits to enhance this feeling include meditation and being present in one's life. These practices help cultivate a deeper sense of vitality and engagement with the world around you.

Resilience, the final element, involves the ability to bounce back when faced with life's challenges. It integrates a spiritual aspect, helping individuals align with a higher being, connect, and grow. Resilience activates hope, enabling one to release negative thoughts and stay focused despite difficulties. The life coach provides tools to avoid distractions, overcome excuses, and develop the capacity to persist through obstacles.

The outcomes of maintaining high energy levels are vast, including feeling alive, remaining engaged, feeling enthusiastic, and living a charged life. Consistency and discipline are crucial to sustaining this momentum.

While there were more sessions on breaking stagnation, the final element I will elaborate on is **psychology**.

In the realm of psychology, the focus is on harnessing the power of the mind and shaping how one thinks and feels. The session covered several key elements of psychology: anxiety, flexibility, happiness, momentum, and connection.

The first area addressed was **anxiety**. While anxiety is a normal emotion that everyone experiences, excessive anxiety can be particularly draining. Extreme anxiety consumes energy and time, depleting one's overall well-being.

People manage anxiety in diverse ways. One effective approach is seeking professional help from a therapist or healthcare provider, demonstrating the courage to ask for assistance to live a more charged life. Another method involves identifying the triggers of one's anxiety. By understanding these triggers, individuals can develop targeted solutions to manage their anxiety effectively.

Additionally, many find relief through spiritual practices. As a Christian, I meditate on the word of God to cope with anxiety. Through prayer and thanksgiving, I believe that divine power intercedes during anxious moments. One of my favorite verses is Philippians 4:6-7, which states:

> *"Do not be anxious about anything, but in every situation, by prayer and petition, with thanksgiving, present your requests to God. And the peace of God, which transcends all understanding, will guard your hearts and your minds in Christ Jesus."*

This verse always brings me peace, and it can do the same for you.

The next element of psychology is **flexibility**. Flexibility is the ability to adapt and flow with life. It begins with one's thinking, emphasizing the importance of having an open mindset rather than a fixed one. Flexibility involves maintaining an open-minded attitude, which is crucial for personal growth, adapting to change, fostering healthy relationships, and achieving success.

The third element of psychology is **momentum**. Momentum is the ability to move forward. Without momentum, progress in one's life is hindered. A life coach can help individuals create momentum to break through stagnation. Maintaining momentum is pivotal for both personal growth and achieving success.

Another key element of psychology is **happiness**. The session began by having individuals rate their overall happiness on a scale of 0-10. According to the life coach, happiness is measured by one's levels of gratitude, joy, appreciation, and satisfaction. Cultivating these positive emotions is essential for a fulfilling and joyful life.

The final element of psychology is **connection**. Connection is the ability to relate to and engage with other people. It is an essential component, especially in relationships. For example, when one is in love, everything seems brighter and more positive because of the strong connection. Conversely, a lack of connection can negatively impact one's psychological well-being. Connection is a crucial measure of one's mental health.

The five elements of psychology—connection, flexibility, happiness, anxiety, and momentum—are pivotal for maintaining a healthy mindset and living an energized life. Other recommended psychological practices include thought-checking, journaling, reframing negative thoughts, identifying personal triggers, and maintaining consistency. These habits and skills help individuals live life more mindfully and proactively. Mastering these practices is essential for optimizing one's mindset and becoming the best version of oneself.

In breaking stagnation, I sought mentorship and discovered a unique program led by Dr. K. N. Jacob, a renowned motivational speaker, mentor, life coach, preacher, and more. This ten-week course covered various essential topics such as mastering your identity, discovering your purpose, self-branding, celebrating your self-image, breaking stagnation in life, and building your legacy. To complement the mentorship program, I also read one of his famous books, *Life Journey: Walk to Your Destiny*.

Each topic in the mentorship program was significant, but one that remains central to my life is **self-branding**. I reflected deeply on my understanding of self-branding, realizing it starts with core values and personal identity. It is about knowing who you are and what you stand for. In the mentorship program, Dr.

Jacob emphasized that your identity is your brand, stating that personal branding is aligning who you are with what you do. He explained that personal branding involves managing your time effectively and is reflected in what people say about you when you are not in the room and how others perceive you.

Personal branding is about being authentic, not pretending to be someone else or comparing yourself to others.

Dr. Jacob further explained that a high-quality brand has three key features: focus, consistency, and character. He concluded with a quote from Mahatma Gandhi: *"The best way to find yourself is to lose yourself in the service of others."* This highlights the importance of knowing that you are the chief executive owner (CEO) of your brand.

In breaking stagnation, I also relocated to a bigger city. I needed to get out of my comfort zone to stretch and grow. Leaving my immediate family, friends, and a community I love was not easy, but I knew there was no more growth or visibility in my familiar environment. I aspired to escape stagnation and tap into my full potential.

I dared to venture into the unknown, hoping to discover where the path would lead. As one motivational speaker says, *"When opportunity meets a prepared mind, the greatest is born."* This move was—and continues to be—a great decision.

REFLECTION

Oh! In self-reflection, breaking stagnation has been a life-changing breakthrough that has fueled me to reach the peaks of my life. The mentorship course and the life coach were instrumental in my personal and professional growth, significantly contributing to overcoming stagnation.

My life continues to be a journey filled with highs and lows. The guidance from my life coach, the mentoring, and the relocation helped me realign to live a more energized life. I demonstrated courage by leaving my comfort zone to venture into the unknown and by seeking mentorship and coaching to break through stagnation.

In this journey, it is critical to write down one's vision and identify the areas that need support to overcome stagnation. Being self-aware and having a clear vision are essential for executing the mission. I continue to implement what I have learned, and every day is an opportunity to emerge as my best version. By consistently breaking through stagnation, I keep reaching new levels.

If you also feel that your life is stagnant, be courageous enough to ask for help, just as I did and continue to do. Embrace the journey of self-improvement and seek the guidance you need to reach your full potential.

Chapter 15

WHOLENESS JOURNEY

On my journey towards wholeness, I discovered that relationships often highlight our broken areas. One cannot achieve wholeness without addressing and mending these broken parts; thus, the process of healing begins. I remember being in a long-term relationship that never flourished into a promising future. After it ended, I found myself in desperate need of radical healing, acceptance, and a sense of completeness.

As an ambitious woman, I had to learn to let go of my fierce independence and pride. I began to surrender to the divine and focus on working through my issues. The first step I took was introspection. I had to look inward and reflect on my past to identify the missing links and understand the root causes of my struggles.

As the late Steve Jobs once said, "You can't connect the dots looking forward; you can only connect them looking backward. So, you must trust that the dots will somehow connect in your future." My process of wholeness started by connecting these dots and committing to the necessary work.

The journey towards wholeness involved thoroughly examining every area of my life to identify the root causes of my brokenness. It required vulnerability and a willingness to scrutinize my patterns. I began by reflecting on my upbringing, which was wonderful. Raised by two loving parents who instilled in us faith, discipline, hard work, and perseverance, my siblings and I learned the importance of working hard and putting God first.

Despite this solid foundation, I realized I needed healing, radical acceptance, and wholeness in two principal areas: recovering from a long-term relationship and reconnecting with my core values and upbringing. Though the relationship had ended, lingering residues of pain required healing. My first step towards wholeness was to cease all contact with my ex, wishing him well but recognizing the need to move on without carrying past residues into my future.

Additionally, I needed to address the drift from my core values and upbringing, which began in my early twenties while attending college. This period marked a deviation from the principles instilled in me during childhood. Reconnecting with these values became essential to my journey of becoming whole.

I began college with a clear focus on my goals. While attending, I made a variety of friends—long-term, social, and seasonal. However, I soon drifted from my core values and upbringing, spending more time with my social friends. I attended parties and occasionally drank. Initially, this lifestyle seemed appealing and fun, attracting certain types of friends.

Despite balancing college, work, and attending church on Sundays, this lifestyle became overwhelming and misaligned with my core values and upbringing. I noticed my grades were declining, and I wasn't performing well in school. I realized I needed to refocus on my goals.

I reached a pivotal point where I disliked the direction my life was heading. Determined to change, I began transitioning away from that lifestyle. It was challenging at first, but I was committed to doing better. As I made that transition, I often found myself alone. I used this solitude to reflect and plan how to restructure my life and aspirations.

Furthermore, my grades gradually improved from Cs to As and Bs. Recognizing the sacrifices my parents made for my siblings and me, I resolved to do better. I often recalled my mother's lessons on self-discipline and moral integrity, principles she had deeply instilled in us.

As I transitioned into my late twenties, I began to live a more purposeful life. I admired the woman I was becoming—someone committed to pursuing her goals and adding value to others. I also attracted friends who shared the same core values.

I knew the process of wholeness would require work, consistency, and patience. I continued working on myself and the healing process, which demanded a deep commitment to self-love. In my research on self-love, I found the author Louise Hay's insights particularly relatable. She explains that self-love is essential before we can truly let anyone else into our lives. It is not selfish but necessary for achieving wholeness.

Louise Hay emphasizes that we often hide our authentic selves, especially after being hurt by past experiences. According to her, self-love begins with being true to oneself. It helps us recognize that we deserve to love ourselves, be loved, and love others. Additionally, self-love requires tender care and nurturing.

As I began working on self-love, I learned that it is vital for any journey towards healing, as it peels away the layers of brokenness. Embracing self-love allowed me to rebuild my sense of self-worth and create a foundation for a more fulfilled and authentic life.

Furthermore, Louise Hay recommended implementing self-love rituals such as daily affirmations and meditation.

Following her advice, I developed a few daily affirmations. One of my self-affirmations was, "I am willing to be open to learning and change." Another was, "My life encompasses love and joy." The final affirmation was, "Today is going to be a great day."

I incorporated these daily affirmations and meditation into my routine. This practice of self-love significantly aided my journey towards wholeness, helping me rebuild my confidence and foster a more positive and loving relationship with myself.

As I continued my journey towards wholeness, I learned five essential elements of a healthy relationship. The first element is having a relationship with God. As a Christian, my identity is rooted in Christ. My siblings and I were raised in a Christian home, but as an adult, I had to acknowledge and take ownership of my failures. I began developing an intimate relationship with God, which involved reading the Word of God, daily devotions, worship songs, and seeking His guidance. This relationship required me to spend less time on social media and be intentional about how I spent my time. Through this intimate journey, I also learned the importance of not compromising my convictions and maintaining high standards.

The second element is openness. Openness requires letting the other person into your life when in a relationship. It demands a willingness to be vulnerable and share both the good and the difficult parts of yourself. This includes being honest about your hurts, desires, and current situations.

The third element is communication. Communication is vital in any relationship, as it allows individuals to express their thoughts, desires, stories, values, and emotions. Effective communication fosters understanding and connection between partners.

The fourth element is wholeness. Wholeness entails healing from inner wounds, past relationships, forgiveness, and being complete with oneself. In my quest for wholeness, I read various books and listened to sermons on the topic. One influential book was *Wholeness* by Pastor Toure Roberts, who states that wholeness begins with acknowledging one's brokenness and surrendering to God. The journey then involves healing, forgiving, and becoming whole. Pastor Toure emphasizes the importance of reminding oneself that you are enough and have enough to be fulfilled, understanding that only the Lord can truly satisfy and complete you.

The work of wholeness requires commitment to the process and patience, as it is a lifelong journey. I also listened to sermons and podcasts that focused on the core message of the Book of Romans, written by Paul. I reread Romans, seeking guidance and wisdom on the subject of wholeness. This book offered empowerment and transformation, consoling me and reminding me of God's goodness. It enriched me with hope and patience for God's timing.

The final element of a healthy relationship is forgiveness and taking ownership. Forgiveness is essential on the journey to wholeness, as it brings peace and liberation. It cleanses the soul and fills one with joy and tranquility.

In my own journey of forgiveness, I had to strive to be Christ-like. Jesus Christ forgives us seventy times seven and is a merciful God. I am grateful for His amazing grace and unconditional love. Embracing forgiveness allowed me to let go of past hurts and move forward with a lighter heart.

Taking ownership of my actions and decisions was also crucial. This meant acknowledging my mistakes, learning from them, and making amends where necessary. It required humility and a willingness to grow.

By integrating these five elements—having a relationship with God, openness, communication, wholeness, and forgiveness—I have laid a strong foundation for healthy relationships and continued my journey towards wholeness. This journey requires work, consistency, and patience, but it leads to a fulfilling and authentic life.

On the other hand, wholeness also involves taking ownership. It means being responsible for your own happiness. I learned that I am responsible for my own joy and fulfillment. True happiness comes from within and is a result of being a whole person.

It is only through living authentic and fulfilling life that one experiences joy. When we embrace our true selves and align our actions with our values, we cultivate inner peace and contentment. True happiness is not found in external achievements alone but in the deep connection we have with ourselves and others. Wholeness comes from accepting both our strengths and imperfections, knowing that growth is a continuous journey. When we live with purpose and gratitude, we unlock a joy that is lasting and deeply rooted within.

Ohh, how the journey of wholeness transformed my life! I transitioned from a place of brokenness to a joyful place. A joyful place of no comparison or resentment. A place of genuine happiness of others such as witnessing my friends as their transitioned from singlehood to getting married or having children. Moreover, the joy of being a bridesmaids to a few of my friend's weddings. These were beautiful transitions and growth mindset, and in hindsight, without the journey towards wholeness, I might not have been as joyful! As Steve Jobs famously said, "Your time is limited, so don't waste it living someone else's life.

This journey teaches the art of delayed gratification and reminds us that life is not instant like a microwave. Like any new birth, growth requires enduring the process. Each step, each challenge, and each victory build the muscle of patience and resilience.

By embracing the slow, deliberate path to wholeness, we learn to savor the journey and value the lessons along the way. This approach helps us cultivate a deeper sense of fulfillment and a more profound appreciation for the journey of life.

REFLECTION

In reflecting on my wholeness journey, I realize the process stretched me beyond my expectations. Along the way, I learned several valuable lessons.

Patience: Wholeness requires patience, much like the growth of a bamboo tree. It is through patiently dissecting the root causes of our pain that the true fruits of our labor become evident. Growth might not be immediately visible, as it takes time for the muscle to stretch and strengthen.

Happiness: True happiness comes from within, and we alone are responsible for our own joy. The journey to wholeness teaches us to take responsibility for our actions and find serenity within ourselves. It underscores the importance of self-love and the realization that we are in charge of our own fulfillment.

Courage: Wholeness demands courage—the courage to acknowledge our brokenness and the willingness to do the work required for healing. It takes the boldness of a lion to admit when we are not okay and to seek guidance and help. Embracing this courage is essential to undertaking the necessary steps toward becoming whole.

Radical Acceptance: This involves accepting the past, the present, and the unknown future. It means doing the work of wholeness to create a new vantage point in life. It also requires the inner courage to leave relationships that drain one's spirit. As a Christian, the process of wholeness reassured me that amid the healing, the Lord was still covering, molding, and stretching me, surpassing my expectations.

In the journey of wholeness, I mended the broken pieces of my life, propelling me to be the best version of myself. This transformative journey is available to everyone, and by embracing these lessons, you too can achieve wholeness and fulfillment.

Chapter 16

RELATIONSHIP

As an author, I dread sharing this phase of my life. I then recalled listening to A ted talk on the power of vulnerability by Brené Brown. Brené Brown is a fantastic author of many books, a researcher, and more. In *The Power of Vulnerability*, she enumerates vital elements of vulnerability. The first facet is connection. She explains that connection is the power of relating to others. She states that one of the factors that hinder connection is shame.

Shame is the feeling that you are not good enough. As I introspected, I realized that the area of my life most affected by shame was my brokenness. The journey to wholeness helped me understand that I am good enough, whether single or in a relationship.

The second facet is the need to feel worthy. After being hurt, it's common to feel unworthy of any connection with others. This hurt can cause one to push people away and build walls to avoid embracing vulnerability.

The final facet is fully embracing vulnerability. Brené Brown discussed that there is power in being seen. Vulnerability means opening your heart and allowing others to see you for who you truly are. In contrast, she explains that when we numb vulnerability due to fear of rejection or hurt, we also numb our joy and happiness.

From Brené Brown's message on the power of vulnerability, I realized the essence of vulnerability in bringing one closer to their audience. The most significant part of vulnerability is being authentic and having the courage to let others see you when sharing your story. Furthermore, vulnerability is vital in any relationship. According to the Macmillan Dictionary, a relationship is "how two or more people or things are connected or involved with each other." There are distinct types of relationships, such as family, sisterhood, brotherhood, business, congregation, partnership, and many more. I will enumerate the power of vulnerability in my relationships.

Here we go! Relationships can bring forth distinct aspects of one's life. The first relationship I witnessed was with my parents. They modeled the art of sticking together through good times and bad. I learned that in any marriage, it takes more than just commitment. One of my desires was to be married and have children.

My first relationship was uniquely different, and I thought it would last a lifetime. Unfortunately, it did not blossom into the future. The end of the relationship was heartbreaking, as I had envisioned a lifetime with that person. We remained friends, but I chose to disconnect all communication to heal. After the breakup, I felt disappointment and brokenness. I decided to take time to heal and become emotionally ready for a new relationship, knowing I did not want to carry past residues into my future.

I became fully aware of my triggers and continued to work on myself. It took several years for me to become whole and healed. I used this time to learn from the relationship and fully recover. Meanwhile, I focused on my visions, career, and travel.

After several years of healing and personal growth, I felt ready to date again. I was open to new relationships. Eventually, I met someone and began dating. Initially, the relationship seemed to be going well, but I soon realized our goals were not aligning, and my intuition fell off. Knowing I did not want to waste my time or someone else's, I took action and ended the relationship. As Maya Angelou says, "When someone shows you who they are, believe them the first time."

I was in a perfect space in my life—whole, confident, and aware of my self-worth. I desired a great friend and life partner whose goals aligned with mine.

I pursued my personal and professional goals while delving into the intricacies of relationships. I vividly remember attending a seminar led by a relationship guru with nearly two decades of marriage experience. He likened relationships to a coin: each person remains independent yet becomes interdependent when together. It was a lot to absorb, but it resonated deeply with me as a relationship dynamic I wanted to explore further. The guru emphasized prioritizing the relationship, growing together while maintaining individuality. In my subsequent relationships, preserving my core identity became paramount; I sought partners who shared a similar commitment to personal growth. I was willing to patiently wait for alignment. Additionally, the guru shared valuable strategies like mindfulness, building resilience, and respecting each other's individuality.

I continued my journey of exploring relationships. Whether traveling, working, or adventuring, I made it a point to engage in conversations with couples, particularly married ones, as that was of interest to me. I would inquire about how they met, what sustained their marriage over the years, and their advice on marriage. The responses were always enlightening and filled with wisdom. Interestingly, I often received the same questions in return: Are you single, married, or dating? My response was always that I am happily single. Their reactions varied from encouraging me to take my time to advising me not to wait too long, to praying for the right partner, emphasizing that marriage takes effort, and suggesting marrying a friend, among other insights.

During these conversations, I had an "aha" moment. As a woman, especially reaching a certain age, societal expectations around marriage and children became more apparent, particularly when I returned to my hometown in Kenya. A significant part of my trip was visiting my 107-year-old grandmother and homeless children in Kenya. Throughout my life, visiting my grandmother has always been a cherished experience. She is vibrant, strong, and filled with stories and humor that I adore. During this particular visit, my family and I spent several hours with her, sharing meals, laughter, and stories. After a while, some of my aunts joined us at my grandmother's home. To my surprise, their first question wasn't about how I was doing or what I had been up to, but rather about my marital status and children.

During my visit, one of my bold aunties went as far as saying, "Just have a child; you don't need a husband or a man!" Initially, I felt the urge to respond with negativity or even use harsh words, but I chose to stay calm and take the high road. Despite this, the day grew more interesting as, several hours later, some cousins, aunties, and uncles boldly asked for money. I boldly responded that I didn't have any money. Their reactions were frustrating; some accused me of feeling superior because I now lived in America, while others implied, I thought I was better than them. Despite this, I chose not to stoop to their level.

The visit with my grandmother eventually ended, and I was grateful to return to my parents' home. I deeply appreciated my parents for their constant support and encouragement. Unlike some relatives, they never pressured me about marriage or having children.

Over time, I've nurtured a supportive inner circle of friends who have consistently uplifted and encouraged me during my lowest moments. Understanding the importance of self-care, I've prioritized filling my own cup so that I can contribute positively to my inner tribe. I deeply cherish the sisterhood and camaraderie within this circle.

My journey in relationships has been joyful, allowing me to blossom into my best self. I've found happiness and fulfillment in life, with aligned goals that push me to grow. These single years are a valuable opportunity for me to fully explore my potential.

I've remained steadfast in not letting others, whether family or friends, impose their expectations on my life. My commitment to personal and professional growth is evident in my dedication to reading and evolving. Recently, I've made significant changes to my daily routine, starting with waking up at 5 a.m. I've established both morning and evening rituals: mornings begin with stretching and light core exercises, followed by devotion and gratitude practice. I then dedicate time to either reading or working on my first book. Exercise and nutrition are integral parts of my day, with intense cardio workouts scheduled two or three times a week based on my agenda. Evenings are reserved for reflection and growth, through reading or engaging in mentorship programs focused on business development.

I've continued to equip myself with strategies for nurturing healthy relationships. Recognizing the emotional nature of being a woman, I've delved into podcasts and teachings on emotional intelligence. To maintain focus, I've deactivated certain social networks and reduced time spent on social media.

Embracing the challenge of rising early and sleeping earlier has significantly increased my productivity. I've learned about the power of mindset and how to activate my reticular activating system (RAS), crucial for driving growth and behavior.

Understanding the importance of morning routines, I strive for consistency while allowing myself grace on days when I fall short. Affirmations have become a powerful tool in my daily life, inspired by figures like Melody, whose affirmations deeply resonate with me. One of my favorites is, "I have a healthy relationship with my season of singlehood and find joy in its purposefulness." This affirmation has reshaped my mindset, boosting my confidence and spiritual growth.

Meditating on these affirmations daily has enriched my soul and strengthened my resolve. I encourage every woman to embrace affirmations that resonate deeply with them, as they have the power to rejuvenate and empower the spirit.

I've continued on my journey of personal growth by seeking counsel, recognizing and addressing emotional and mental traumas that may have affected me knowingly or unknowingly. Understanding the concept of blind spots from a philosopher in a documentary, I realized the importance of external guidance in overcoming them. Inspired by the philosopher's transformation through a life coach, I decided to seek counsel from a life coach myself.

Having previously attended sessions with this particular life coach, I appreciate his unique approach, characterized by honesty, sincerity, and a genuine concern for others' well-being. His success in various areas, such as marriage, authorship, and speaking, further affirmed my decision. I found safety, liberation, and clarity in our coaching sessions, which always began and ended with prayer, aligning with my Christian faith and creating a synergistic environment for growth.

In each coaching session, I've gained new perspectives on relationships and self-discovery. I've found clarity, developed a new mindset, and gained assurance that I'm on the right path after each session. My life coach emphasized the power of gathering information through meaningful conversations, being innovative, and discerning potential scams that target women. I've also learned the importance of following each step in a relationship process without skipping ahead.

As a dedicated student and attentive listener, I've applied these lessons with positive results. Maintaining an open mindset has been crucial in my journey of personal and professional evolution.

Taking risks has also been instrumental in my growth journey. In my quest to try new things, I've ventured into salsa dancing, something I've always wanted to learn. Despite initial challenges in learning the steps, the experience has been exciting and fulfilling.

Oh, I'm deeply grateful for my journey in relationships and the woman I am continually evolving into. I'm also thankful for the women of faith who consistently pray for me. One profound aspect of strengthening my faith is through fasting and prayer. Through fasting and prayer, I build spiritual resilience, strengthening my connection with God and deepening my intimacy with Him, seeking guidance from the Holy Spirit while diminishing the influence of worldly desires.

Conversely, I've come to understand the power of courage in vulnerability within relationships. It involves acknowledging emotional imbalances, working through them, and emerging from a place of inner peace. It requires committing to the necessary emotional maturity, mastering the art of effective communication, and facing challenges head-on rather than avoiding or escaping from them.

In this journey of relationships, I've embraced the belief that when I align myself with who I am meant to be and trust in the process, I will naturally attract the right person, akin to the Law of Attraction.

REFLECTION

Dear Younger Self,

The first step is learning to love yourself fully, knowing that you are more than enough. Embrace vulnerability- it is not a weakness but a strength, as Brené Brown teaches. love without guarantees and practice grati-tude in every season of life.

As you grow, dare to be vulnerable. Let others see your true self while cultivating joy. Raise your standards, knowing that the right people will appreciate your worth-flaws and all. Your authenticity is your power. Laugh often, cherish the little moments, and surround yourself with a supportive tribe that celebrates you. Trust your intuition;it will always guide you to the right path.

Remember, when people show you who they truly are, believe them the first time. Let failures propel you forward-take risks, strive for better, and never settle. Work on understanding your emotions, especially your triggers, and strive for emotional maturity.

Embrace reality and continue evolving. Release anything or anyone unworthy of your time and energy. You are on the right path, attracting those who recognize your rarity, worth, and brilliance-just like a precious ruby.

With love and wisdom,
Your Older Self

Chapter 17

MY ENTREPRENEURIAL JOURNEY

My journey into entrepreneurship was nothing like I had imagined myself, a path filled with unexpected turns, moments of both turbulence and deep fulfillment. Looking back, I can see how each step, even the difficult ones, carried me toward a more authentic and purpose-driven life.

Growing up, my vision was conventional: excel in school, secure impressive grades, and land a stable career in healthcare or finance. I believed the traditional formula—good education leads to a respectable job, which guarantees financial security. This mindset guided me straight into medical science, where I specialized in nursing.

With my Bachelor of Science in Nursing in hand, I began working at a Level One Trauma Hospital. The next decade saw me serving in various healthcare roles, each position adding invaluable experience and shaping me in ways I couldn't have anticipated. I remain profoundly grateful for the skills and growth this season provided.

My career evolved further after earning my graduate degree as a Family Nurse Practitioner. This qualification opened doors to diverse settings—outpatient primary care, travel nursing, telehealth, and acute care. Then came 2020, when COVID-19 transformed healthcare globally. While the pandemic created unprecedented challenges, it also revealed new possibilities. Telehealth expanded rapidly, and nurses were suddenly in extraordinary demand worldwide. It was against this backdrop of disruption and opportunity that my entrepreneurial vision began to take shape.

Uncertain how to proceed with this emerging vision, I sought guidance from one of my most trusted mentors, my elder sister. While supportive, she wisely advised me to seek expertise from someone established within healthcare entrepreneurship. Despite my growing aspirations, I maintained my full-time position, grateful for its stability yet increasingly aware of its limitations. The predictable rhythm of depending on bi-weekly paychecks left me yearning for greater freedom and the chance to realize my full potential.

Within a year, I made a significant move to a larger city. The excitement of relocating to an unfamiliar environment was both invigorating and frightening, particularly the prospect of losing my job. When I informed my manager about the move, her response surprised me. She valued my work ethic, reliability, and team spirit too much to lose me as an employee. Instead of accepting my resignation, she offered the opportunity to continue working via telehealth. This unexpected flexibility reinforced an important lesson: not letting fear limit my potential.

The transition to my new city proceeded smoothly, thanks in part to my cousin who hosted me during this adjustment period. Through a series of networking connections that began with my mother introducing me to her friend, who then introduced me to her friend, I met someone whose values and ethics aligned remarkably with my vision. Over several months, we built mutual trust and rapport.

I remember vividly when she proposed venturing into the homecare agency business. The idea resonated with me immediately, though I chose to keep my own vision private until our relationship deepened. As our conversations about the business continued, she revealed she had already formed her own homecare agency and expressed interest in a partnership. This opportunity excited me—I was ready to be a business partner rather than merely an employee.

The next milestone was preparing for the state survey, a crucial step to begin servicing clients. Our combined skills and qualifications complemented each other's strengths and weaknesses perfectly. We agreed on a fifty-fifty partnership covering both expenditures and profit distribution, including sharing responsibility for repaying the business's starting capital. My partner mentioned her accountant could draft our operating agreement, and I agreed, optimistic about our future collaboration.

However, this marked the beginning of unexpected challenges. While both maintaining our previous jobs, we simultaneously worked on growing the business—developing marketing strategies, administrative systems, software solutions, and operational plans. My partner introduced me to one of her friends who successfully operated her own private homecare business, providing us with valuable insights into the industry's day-to-day realities.

We continued preparing for the state survey, a critical step for any homecare business. I assisted my partner with the necessary paperwork and safety requirements, ensuring we met all regulatory standards. As the survey date approached, our anxiety heightened naturally. The day arrived, and thanks to our thorough preparation, we passed successfully. The excitement of this achievement was palpable—we were now ready to begin serving clients.

That evening remains vivid in my memory. Exhausted from our business meeting, I tucked the partnership agreement away, planning to review it later. When I finally read through it before sunrise the next morning, my heart sank. The written terms bore little resemblance to what we had verbally agreed upon. The discrepancies weren't minor. They fundamentally altered our partnership structure. My initial reaction was one of betrayal and anger, but I knew making decisions from this emotional state would only compound the problem.

Instead, I stepped back to collect myself and sought wisdom from trusted sources—family members with business experience and legal advisors who understood partnership law. Armed with their counsel and a clearer perspective, I reached out to my partner the following day. Despite my hopes for resolution, our conversation revealed an uncomfortable truth: our visions for the business had diverged beyond reconciliation.

This realization was painful. I had poured my time, energy, and expertise into building this venture from the ground up. Yet rather than allowing this setback to derail my entrepreneurial journey, I made the difficult but liberating decision to venture forward independently. Stepping away from the partnership brought an unexpected gift—a sense of clarity and renewed purpose. Without the complications of misaligned expectations, I could now focus entirely on building a business that truly reflected my values and vision.

As Tony Gaskins wisely noted, "If you don't build your dream, someone will hire you to help build theirs." Despite the setback, my vision continued propelling forward. My mother's reassurance, "Your help comes from the Lord" strengthened my resolve. Leaning on my core values of faith and resilience, I adjusted course and prepared to soar, deeply grateful for my inner circle's unwavering support.

One evening while browsing YouTube, I discovered a confident woman discussing successful entrepreneurship in homecare. Her authenticity and expertise resonated with me, and I learned she was a business coach. Refusing to let fear overshadow my vision, I researched her background and eventually contacted her secretary to schedule a coaching session. This decision proved to be one of my wisest investments. Working with Coach Michele has been, and continues to be, invaluable to my business development.

They say, "Success occurs when opportunity meets preparation." My prior exposure to the business world, though challenging, prepared me for independent entrepreneurship. I enrolled in a comprehensive coaching program, determined to build a successful, vision-driven business. Understanding that significant achievement requires support, I felt fortunate to surround myself with the right guidance and community. The coaching program established a solid foundation for my business journey.

"Don't aspire to make a living; aspire to make a difference." These words from Denzel Washington perfectly capture the deeper purpose behind my entrepreneurial vision—not just to build a business, but to create a lasting legacy of positive impact.

This expanded vision crystallized during a pivotal trip to Kenya with my mother and elder sister. The journey began with my mother's compassionate heart. After seeing a YouTube video about homeless children in Kenya, she didn't just feel moved—she felt called to action. She proposed we visit these children as a family, reaching out to friends to help with food preparation while my middle sister collected clothing donations from her network.

On that transformative Saturday, we arrived at a modest home run by a remarkable 63-year-old woman who had dedicated her life to sheltering homeless children. Walking through the small dwelling that housed sixty-one children, I was struck by both the simplicity of the conditions and the magnitude of this woman's commitment. Children shared beds due to space limitations, and even the caretaker herself shared her room with two children. Most heartbreaking were the babies with severe disorders, including spinal cord injuries, receiving care with such limited resources.

As I served meals to these children, something profound shifted within me. This wasn't just about charity—it was about applying entrepreneurial thinking to create sustainable solutions. The experience connected directly to my business journey, showing me how the same skills that build companies can address humanitarian challenges.

Upon returning to the United States, my sister and I channeled our business acumen into action. We created a GoFundMe campaign with specific targets and timelines, leveraged our professional networks for support, and contributed our own resources. The response was overwhelming—we nearly reached our ambitious funding goal, securing enough resources to ensure these children wouldn't go hungry for at least a year.

This experience became the foundation for my non-profit organization, BEACON OF LIGHT. More importantly, it revealed how entrepreneurship can be a vehicle for social change—demonstrating that the same skills that build successful businesses can create meaningful impact in our world's most vulnerable communities.

I'm deeply grateful to everyone who joined us in this effort—the women who generously gave their time and service, my mother for illuminating this path, my middle sister for her clothing donations and network mobilization, and my elder sister and childhood friend for their participation. From this initial visit to homeless children and orphans, a new path emerged, and a legacy began taking shape.

As Mother Teresa wisely observed, "Not all of us can do great things. But we can do small things with great love." Inspired by this philosophy, I established a non-profit organization dedicated to feeding children and empowering people of all genders. I invite you to visit my foundation, BEACON OF LIGHT, at www.beaconoflight.com. Together, we truly can become beacons of light in this world.

Throughout my entrepreneurial journey, several key factors have contributed to my progress. Perhaps the most fundamental was a profound shift in mindset. Your mental framework is crucial when pivoting into entrepreneurship. I deliberately cultivated an abundance mindset by immersing myself in content about millionaire habits and thought patterns. These resources helped me transform my perspective and integrate daily affirmations that boosted my self-confidence and intentionality.

I created specific abundance affirmations to recite daily: "I will be a giver, not a borrower," "I will be successful in my business," and "I am worthy of having more than enough." Consistently implementing these practices has established the psychological foundation for my entrepreneurial path.

Another critical element was embracing the art of giving. A memorable lesson from a motivational speaker emphasized that charitable giving is essential for achieving abundance. By prioritizing charity, volunteering, and community contribution, I discovered that giving keeps one humble and grounded—and surprisingly, creates space for receiving. Moving from a scarcity to an abundance mindset through giving has continually expanded my horizons and strengthened my community connections.

The final essential habit has been continuous learning and personal growth. This involves regular reading, research, podcast listening, and conference attendance. I particularly invest in two transformative conferences annually: a homecare entrepreneur conference and a leadership conference.

The homecare entrepreneur conference organized by Coach Michele offers far more than industry information—it provides genuine life transformation. Coach Michele and her team assemble diverse experts who ignite attendees' dreams and transform their perspectives. I invariably leave feeling profoundly inspired. During one conference, Coach Michele used the dolphin as a powerful metaphor for entrepreneurship—explaining how these intelligent creatures, like successful entrepreneurs, adapt quickly, innovate around obstacles, build strong teams, respond gracefully to challenges, and demonstrate remarkable resilience. Though dolphins start slowly, they eventually gain tremendous momentum—perfectly symbolizing the entrepreneurial journey. Coach Michele emphasizes that entrepreneurial success fundamentally stems from the mindset, prioritizing excellent service with humility, which naturally attracts financial rewards.

The International Leadership Conference, founded by Bishop T.D. Jakes and his team, has become another cornerstone of my professional development. While grounded in Christian principles, this conference welcomes attendees from all faiths and backgrounds. One conference remains etched in my memory, where the theme centered on leaders as "master builders"—inspired by the passage from Galatians: "As a wise master builder, I have laid the foundation, and another buildeth thereon."

Bishop Jakes outlined the seasons every master builder must navigate:

The Foundation Season: This initial period focuses on preparation of incubation, molding, learning, and relearning. For entrepreneurs, this means immersing ourselves in our industry through seminars, books, mentorship, and developing systems that will support our vision. As both an entrepreneur and author, I recognize this as my current season, a time to build the knowledge base and structural framework that will support future growth.

The Level-Setting Season: Once the foundation is established, we enter a period of disciplined implementation. This season demands the right mindset—shifting from planning to execution, from theory to practice. During level-setting, we create order, establish structure, and follow systems. This is where I'm learning to align strategy with vision and accepting that success unfolds through process rather than overnight transformation.

Bishop Jakes emphasizes several powerful principles for master builders:

- Where God starts, He continues
- Understanding the deal enables you to execute the deal
- God is waiting for YOUR action
- Building according to pattern (like Noah)
- The importance of both modeling and mentoring

These principles remind me that entrepreneurial success requires both divine inspiration and disciplined implementation, a partnership between vision and execution that transforms ideas into reality. Through systems, accountability, and consistent action, the level-setting season transforms our raw potential into tangible results.

Dr. K.N. Jacob's book, "You Don't Need a Job You Were Designed to Work Not, Not Be Employed", has also profoundly influenced my entrepreneurial perspective. He uses the powerful analogy that ships are safest at dock but aren't built to remain there indefinitely. This metaphor resonated deeply as I recognized my own "safe harbor" had been the predictability of a steady paycheck. True entrepreneurship requires sailing into unfamiliar waters, away from the safety of shore.

Dr. Jacob discusses breaking free from the "prison mentality" that employment is the only path to financial security. His recommendations include mastering your time and life, believing in your talents, developing a financial transition plan, maintaining accountability relationships, and exercising faith coupled with action. He emphasizes that "greatness precedes faith" believing in future success while taking concrete steps toward it today.

The book highlights several qualities of successful entrepreneurs that I've worked to cultivate: a winning mindset (reinforced through my daily affirmations), self-belief (confidence in my abilities while seeking help when needed), strong personal branding (continuously developing my professional identity), effective networking (regularly connecting with mentors and industry colleagues), persistence (refusing to surrender despite obstacles), resilience (rebuilding after setbacks), and fearlessness (stretching beyond comfort zones).

I've implemented many of Dr. Jacob's principles in my own journey, beginning with releasing my attachment to the "safe harbor" mentality. This required honest financial assessment and developing a transition plan before resigning from my full-time position. It demanded financial discipline and unwavering commitment to my vision.

I've also embraced the understanding that entrepreneurial success requires patience—staying the course despite obstacles or delayed profits. I continue following my mentors' guidance, investing in coaching, seeking wise counsel, and drawing strength from my core values of faith and resilience. With this winning mindset, I continue growing both as an entrepreneur and as a person.

This journey—filled with both fulfillment and uncertainty—continues to be a marvelous adventure that I wouldn't trade for any amount of predictability or safety. Each day brings new challenges and opportunities that confirm I'm exactly where I'm meant to be, building something meaningful that extends far beyond myself.

REFLECTION

In my entrepreneurship journey, it continues to be a groundbreaking paradigm shift from being employed to self-employed. I am still learning, stretching, and evolving. Here are the lessons I've learned on this path:

1. **Taking Charge of Your Destiny**

    Despite the turbulence on the path, you are the captain of your ship. Take charge and navigate through challenges with confidence.

2. **Gratitude**

    Journaling daily about things that went well and what you're grateful for creates positivity and great synergy.

A gratitude journal fosters a positive outlook and helps maintain focus on the good.

3. **Counsel**

   Surround yourself with the right counsel and people who tell you the truth. Be intentional about your environment and the people you associate with. Surrounding yourself with like-minded individuals is crucial.

4. **Being a Quick Learner**

   Business is highly competitive. To stay on top, you must learn quickly and efficiently, finding out what differentiates you from other companies.

5. **Service**

   Serving others is essential—give back to the community, uplift others, volunteer your time, and be a resource. Service creates a positive impact and builds lasting relationships.

6. **Growth of Your Business**

   Continuous learning and skill mastery are key to business growth. Attending conferences, reading extensively, and networking to stretch and expand your horizons.

7. **Learning from Failures**

   Do not let failures define your success. Learn from them and let them lead you to the next opportunity. Embrace failures as steppingstones to greater achievements.

This new path of entrepreneurship has been a joyful journey. As Lou Holtz says, "In this world, you're either growing or you're dying, so get in motion and grow." I plan on continuing to stay in motion, stretch, and grow, and I encourage you to do the same!

To all the tribe that has guided me on this journey, I am forever grateful. To my mentors, coaches, role models, accountability partners, family, and everyone who has encouraged me, I say thank you.

Chapter 18

THE POWER OF YOUR VOICE

In my quest to emerge as my best version, I rediscovered the power of one's voice. It is a unique place where one discovers an inner strength that supersedes outward appearances. I will enumerate certain scenarios that illustrate the power of my voice.

The first realization of the power of my voice started in my final year of high school after relocating to the United States. As I continued my academics, I frequently encountered the question, "Where are you from?" or "Where is your accent from?" Initially, these questions were irritating. It took me a while to muster the courage to answer boldly. I realized that my accent and origins are part of my identity, grounding me. It became an opportunity to represent my ancestors and the people who fought for our independence from British colonial rule.

Moreover, it gave me pride to know that I come from strong men and women who fought for my freedom and the chance for an education. I realized that there is power in my voice; whenever I speak, I represent my identity, forefathers, and culture.

The next realization came through understanding my personality. In my limited knowledge, I believed one needed a huge personality and a bold demeanor to make a difference. However, a self-discovery journey revealed the power of my true personality. As an introvert, I don't need to be loud or talkative to convey a point. I can be myself, with poise and grace, to address concerns or engage in conversation. This poised confidence was liberating.

In reviewing an article, I realized that historically, numerous successful introverts have made significant impacts, such as Warren Buffet, Abraham Lincoln, Mahatma Gandhi, and Mark Zuckerberg, to name a few.

These realizations underscore the power of embracing one's authentic voice and personality. It is through this self-acceptance and confidence that true strength and influence emerge.

Why Introverts Make Great Leaders

1. **Poised Personality**

   Introverts' calm and collected demeanor can be reassuring and inspiring to others.

2. **Character, Trust, and Integrity**

   Introverts often exhibit strong moral principles, building trust and integrity within their teams.

3. **Ability to Listen Without Interrupting**

   Introverts listen deeply to others' concerns before making conclusions, leading to more thoughtful and informed decisions.

4. **Energy from Serenity and Solitude**

   Introverts gain energy from quiet and reflective environments, which can foster creativity and strategic thinking.

5. **Critical Thinking**
   Introverts tend to be critical thinkers, which can lead to innovative solutions and opportunities.

In today's world, where instant gratification is common, the introvert's ability to slow down and reflect can lead to better decision-making and more meaningful interactions. Embracing these qualities has empowered me to grow as a leader and an individual.

In contrast, there are some skills that introverts can enhance to be better leaders. One important skill is the ability to make quick decisions, especially in emergencies. Another enhancement for introverts is learning to engage with large crowds by surrounding themselves with extroverts for stimulation and avoiding isolation. Realizing the need to enhance these skills was a light-bulb moment, highlighting the importance of growing as a person and a leader while embracing my introverted personality.

Another realization of the power of my voice came from my quiet confidence. I recall a particular summer when I had a court case. At the time, I was a full-time student pursuing my undergraduate degree and working full-time. My finances were limited, and every penny was accounted for and budgeted. I found myself in a court case and could not afford a lawyer. Additionally, I was unfamiliar with the law and how to represent myself. The only thing that kept me going was my quiet confidence.

As the court date approached, my nerves grew. I had a lengthy conversation with my mother about my court case. She had worked for a law firm for several years and was familiar with the court system. Aware of my hectic schedule and limited legal knowledge, she commended me for my bravery and advised me on specific points that occur during court proceedings and the formalities to expect. She assured me that, no matter the outcome, she was proud of me.

Her advice and support reinforced my quiet confidence, allowing me to face the court case with composure and determination. This experience further solidified my understanding of the power of my voice and the strength found in my introverted nature.

The court date finally dawned, and my nerves were at their peak. The hearing was scheduled for the evening, and the previous night and morning were sleepless due to overwhelming anxiety. I did my best to calm myself, gathering all necessary documents and preparing for the case. I also ensured to eat a heavy meal in the morning and lunch to keep my energy up and avoid fainting in court.

The court proceedings began in the evening and lasted for an hour before adjourning. In the last twenty minutes, the judge delivered the final judgment. Unfortunately, I lost the case, but I will never forget the judge's remark: "You are one brave young lady!" This experience taught me the power of my voice, even in the face of uncertainty and failure. The lessons learned during that time strengthened the muscle within the power of my voice.

Another realization of the power of my voice came during my entrepreneurial journey. Initially, I believed that a partnership was the only path to business success. However, through personal and professional growth, I realized that having a talented team and a reliable system is what truly matters. I learned to speak up for myself whenever I found myself in an unfair partnership, leading me to establish my business as a sole proprietorship. As a businesswoman, I navigated uncertainty and harnessed the power of my voice to advocate for myself and my vision.

Through these experiences, I discovered that the power of one's voice is not just about speaking up, but also about embodying courage, resilience, and self-assurance. Embracing these qualities has allowed me to grow both personally and professionally, making my journey truly fulfilling.

Furthermore, I would listen to podcasts and motivational speakers like Les Brown. Les Brown emphasizes principles necessary for success in life. One of these principles is to surround oneself with quality people. Other principles include patience, persistence, and maintaining a positive attitude. I was determined to apply these principles in my entrepreneurial journey.

Forming the homecare agency required immense patience. I learned to be patient with myself, others, and the business process while maintaining a positive attitude. Business itself demanded persistence through the good, the bad, and the unknown. I continue to implement Les Brown's three P's to navigate business uncertainty effectively.

Les Brown also discussed the importance of surrounding oneself with quality people. This insight prompted me to introspect the friends and people I was surrounding myself with. Consequently, I repositioned my inner circle, mentors, and established accountability partners for my business. I realized the vitality of a positive mindset and the power of my voice in business.

The final realization of the power of my voice came during a seminar on psychology. Psychology is crucial as it aids in understanding how and why we think or feel a certain way. At the workshop, the instructor discussed different themes of identity and the four elements of psychology.

1. **Cue**

   A cue is a feeling or signal that something will happen next. Cues can be positive or negative. According to the instructor, developing a cue that helps our mind become more conscious in practicing habits, such as thought checking, is vital.

2. **Conditioning**

   Conditioning is the automatic programming of oneself. It involves rewiring oneself with good behavior to replace unhealthy habits or routines. Conditioning helps with mental stamina and can be trained. Cues and conditioning are interchangeable: cues signal that something is about to happen, while conditioning triggers those emotions.

3. **Consequence**

   A consequence is the outcome of a goal, which can be either positive or negative. For example, a positive consequence might be celebrating after achieving a specific target goal. It's a learning process to condition oneself to obtain the desired consequence.

4. **Choice**

   Choice is the ability to make a conscious decision. As adults, we learn to intentionally create choices that will move us to the next level. The seminar's session on these four elements of psychology was enlightening. I continue to implement the lessons learned in psychology by taking charge of my thoughts and navigating the power of my voice.

Another element of psychology covered in the seminar was various themes of identity. The instructor discussed five distinctive themes, which are declarations of evolving: "I am deserving," "I am ready," "I am capable," "I am open," "I am persistent," and "I am a role model." According to the instructor, these five declarations propel one to the next level.

1. **I am deserving**

   This theme emphasizes that one deserves remarkable things and fosters a sense of worth. It is about giving oneself permission to declare that you are good enough.

2. **I am ready**

   This declaration signifies being prepared for opportunities and challenges, indicating a mindset of readiness for what lies ahead.

3. **I am capable**

   Acknowledging one's abilities and strengths is crucial. This theme instills confidence in one's skills and talents.

4. **I am open**

   Being open to new experiences, ideas, and growth is vital for continuous personal and professional development.

5. **I am persistent**

   Persistence is key to overcoming obstacles and achieving long-term goals. This theme encourages resilience and determination.

6. **I am a role model**

   Recognizing oneself as a role model inspires accountability and motivates others through one's actions and achievements.

These declarations have significantly influenced my approach to personal and professional growth. By embracing these themes, I continue to harness the power of my voice and mindset, ensuring that I evolve and progress on my entrepreneurial journey. Implementing these lessons has allowed me to navigate challenges with a clear sense of purpose and direction, reinforcing the importance of psychology in shaping one's identity and success.

REFLECTION

Reflecting on the power of my voice has been a unique and enlightening experience. It has allowed me to recognize my inner strength and how it reflects externally, while also teaching me continuous life lessons.

Embracing My Personality While Enhancing My Skills

One of the key lessons has been embracing my personality while enhancing my skills. As an introvert, I've learned to value my quiet confidence and the strengths that come with it. At the same time, I've recognized the importance of developing skills that complement my natural tendencies, such as making quick decisions and engaging with larger crowds when necessary.

The Courage to Share My Story and Pursue My Dreams

Another significant lesson is the courage to share my story and pursue my dreams. Whether it's starting my own business or speaking up in challenging situations, I've learned that my voice matters and can inspire others.

Speaking Up with My Unique Accent

Having the courage to speak up with my unique accent has been a profound realization. My accent is part of my identity, representing the strong men and women who fought for my freedom. Embracing this aspect of myself has given me a sense of pride and connection to my heritage.

Surrounding Myself with Quality People
Surrounding myself with quality people and implementing key principles in life has been instrumental in my growth. By aligning myself with mentors, accountability partners, and like-minded individuals, I've created a supportive environment that fosters continuous improvement.

Using My Voice to Contribute to the World
Finally, a pivotal lesson has been using my voice to contribute to the world. Through the power of my voice, I add value to myself, others, and the world at large. It's about finding your unique rhythm and confidently expressing it.

In summary, the power of my voice has not only helped me grow personally and professionally but also allowed me to make meaningful contributions. It is an ongoing journey of self-discovery and empowerment, where each lesson learned reinforces the significance of speaking up and staying true to oneself.

Chapter 19

THE PEAK OF MY LIFE

Reaching the Peak of My Life

Oh, the exhilaration of reaching the peak of my life as I evolved into my best version! This journey has been filled with leaps of faith and abundant joy, brimming with vitality amid the unknown. It feels like just yesterday when I realized the importance of leaving the confines of my comfort zone to discover hidden potentials and gifts.

The peak of my life is a grand haven, marked by visible growth and self-awareness. One of the most significant areas of growth has been gratitude. My life overflows with gratitude for life itself, the victories and lessons learned, the failures, and the unknown. I no longer compare myself to others' fortunes, friends, lives, or families. As Theodore Roosevelt wisely said, "Comparison is the thief of joy." My life is now filled with inward and outward fulfillment.

One of the pivotal peaks was leaving my safe harbor. Deep inside, I knew it was the right season to take this step. Despite not knowing exactly how to navigate the journey, I took a leap of faith, committed to giving it my all. As I drove on the highway to return the rental car and keys, I felt a profound stillness.

It was my last contract job, marking the end of helping build someone else's empire. I was ready to steer the ship of my own empire as a sole proprietor and entrepreneur. There was a sense of tranquility that was more profound than usual.

Furthermore, I was struggling with a headache from the stress of the unknown. As my elder sister arrived to pick me up, I could sense an intangible shift within me. She seemed to feel the energy too. She invited me to one of her favorite places to eat. To create harmony and boost my confidence in facing the unknown, we went to the restaurant, ordered our dinner, and then proceeded to our seats. I intentionally chose a seat with dim light to avoid aggravating my headache. Spontaneously, she broke the ice with hilarious humor. At that moment, I realized it was real. There was no more reliance on bi-weekly or weekly salaries; I was in a different world now. I had stepped out of my comfort zone and into the uncertainty zone. I was determined to seize this window of opportunity.

As it says in the Book of Proverbs, "There is safety in the multitude of counsel." With the guidance of my personal and professional mentors, I was well-equipped with a solid foundation. On the other hand, I was willing to navigate through the unknown. It is the best yet most fulfilling risk I dare to undertake.

Another pivotal moment was navigating public speaking. During my undergraduate studies, I had to take a public communication class as a prerequisite for my major. As an introvert, I felt extremely nervous and shy. Each assignment required a presentation in front of the students and the teacher, and each presentation was nerve-wracking. I had negative thoughts telling me I wasn't good enough, that no one could understand my accent, and I lacked confidence. Because of this fear, I failed the class the first time, unable to present my final project.

I had a long discussion with my mother about my fear of public speaking. She advised me to start practicing in front of the mirror, to see myself as I spoke, and to stand up straight with proper posture. Determined to face my fears, I decided to try again. I began practicing reluctantly in front of the mirror for each assignment or presentation. Initially, it felt awkward, but with each practice session, something began to shift. I started with affirmations like, "I am a lion and can do anything," before proceeding with my presentation.

With continued practice in front of the mirror, I built my confidence. I retook the class and passed with an A-. I was immensely grateful for my mother's advice, which significantly boosted my self-confidence. The introverted girl was learning to overcome her fears. I completed my undergraduate and graduate studies, passing all presentation courses. I continue to use affirmations and practice presentations in front of the mirror, reinforcing the skills I developed.

As an adult, one of my hobbies is reading books. I recall reading Mel Robbins's book, *The High 5 Habit*. Mel Robbins is a motivational speaker, author, and lawyer. She explains the essentials of simple habits, such as the High 5, which are supported by research. She states that high fiving yourself in the mirror every day is a vital act. By doing this simple action, you are telling yourself you are worthy, acknowledging your feelings, and learning to celebrate. Practicing these simple acts builds inner strength rather than focusing on external validation.

One of the chapters in the book resonated deeply with the advice my mother gave me about practicing presentations in front of the mirror. Mel Robbins's book provided the proven research and science behind why high fiving yourself in the mirror works. A decade later, my mother's advice was backed by evidence. The introverted girl I once was has transformed, acquiring tools to overcome her fears.

Over the years, I have had the opportunity to host friends' events and give public presentations. I continue to receive more opportunities to host church and community events. It doesn't come easy, but to grow, one must embrace discomfort and inconvenience. I now celebrate my uniqueness, beautiful accent, differences, and flaws. At my core, I know I am worthy, good enough, and marvelous. Moreover, I appreciate other people's uniqueness, differences, and flaws more than ever.

Another significant moment at the peak of my life is integrating habits that elevate me to the next level. Some of these habits include waking up before dawn, reading books, traveling, and cultivating a powerful mindset. As I continue to evolve, I intentionally read thought-provoking books, dedicating time to read a chapter at least three or four times a week. A few of my favorite books that I highly recommend are *The 5 AM Club* by Robin Sharma, *The High 5 Habit* by Mel Robbins, *Choosing to Prosper* by Bola Sokunbi, and *Disruptive Thinking* by T.D. Jakes.

In Sharma's *The 5 AM Club*, he expounds that the secret of success goes beyond arduous work. The secret lies in "forming the habit of doing things that failures don't like to do." This insight has been profoundly impactful. The knowledge in these books has played a pivotal role in my life, propelling me to the next level.

Another source of immense joy for me is my love of travel. My journey has led me to explore diverse destinations across the United States, the vibrant cities of my homeland, Kenya, the captivating culture of Mexico, the modern marvels of the United Arab Emirates (UAE),the serene beauty of Zanzibar, and the breathtaking landscapes of Australia.

Each travel experience has been a unique blend of enrichment and adventure, leaving me with cherished memories and a deeper appreciation for the world's diversity.

During one of my international travels to the UAE, the trip was filled with numerous adventures. It began with the distinct hospitality of the Emirati people and their exceptional customer service. I admired Sheikh Zayid's vision to transform a desert into a vibrant country, with its remarkable infrastructure and creativity, epitomized by the Burj Khalifa.

The adventure continued with a desert safari, exploring the desert in SUVs, cruising up and down the dunes, and stopping to witness a breathtaking sunset. The evening was filled with cultural experiences, including local cuisine and belly dancing. The night ended with stargazing, marveling at the vastness of the universe and the masterful creation surrounding us.

I am still pursuing my joy of traveling, especially internationally, to Europe and other continents. There is a rare mystery about travel that expands one's horizons. Learning about other cultures and ways of life gives one a new perspective. It keeps you grounded and always a student of life.

Oh, the power of one's mindset! As Warren Buffet says, "The poor invest in money while the rich invest in time." It's about learning to shift one's perspective. Understanding that time is one of the most precious commodities is crucial. Hence, it's essential to strategize in life by guarding your mind and letting positive energy flow throughout the day. It's also about having tools to overcome negative thoughts or fears.

Another transformative habit is rising early before dawn. During the early hours, one can focus and generate great ideas. Winning your morning with inner peace and a renewed mind sets the tone for the rest of the day. Additionally, developing daily rituals helps maintain momentum.

Another peak of my life is the vitality of exercise. In my twenties, I could maintain a healthy weight with minimal effort. However, when I entered my thirties, the challenge began. It became essential to establish a routine exercise regimen. On days when I don't feel like running or going to the gym, I push myself to exercise regardless. It's about pushing through despite my feelings, physical soreness, or aches. The reward comes later when my mind is clear, and my productivity reaches new heights. Aligning my goals to strive for holistic health has been key.

To keep the exercise momentum going, I have formulated certain habits. One of them includes laying my gym clothes next to my bed, ensuring they are the first thing I see in the morning. Another practice is high-fiving myself in the mirror, which helps me celebrate myself and stay centered. Daily affirmations are also crucial, helping maintain a positive mindset and energy. These habits keep me grounded and motivated. I incorporate variety into my exercise routines, such as running, cycling, and weight training, to keep my body challenged. Additionally, I have accountability partners who motivate and push each other. Exercise reduces brain fog, improves brain health, lowers disease risk, and enhances productivity.

The final peak of my life is the power of one's inner circle. As I continue to evolve, so do my inner circle and friendships. I've learned the art of guarding my heart, creating a haven where only certain people have the privilege of entry. Friendships come in different forms: some are seasonal, others lifelong, and some uncertain. It's crucial to discern the distinct types of friendships, whether comrades, constituents, or confidants. Additionally, it's important to communicate your boundaries while respecting others' boundaries.

Throughout my journey, I have had the privilege of experiencing all three types of friendships. Some lifelong friendships date back to childhood, high school, college, and now as an adult. Friendship is similar to the law of attraction: one has to be a great friend to attract a great friend.

On the other hand, my inner circle is unique. We mutually fill each other's cups, adding value, building trust, and genuinely wanting the best for one another without malice. My journey encompasses openness, challenges, drifts, inner peace, and uncertainty. I am relearning to celebrate my wins, encouraging and motivating myself and those around me each day. Additionally, I am rediscovering the importance of radiating positive energy to myself, others, and the environment. I continue to align my life, stretch my potential, and strive to become my best version, and so can you!

REFLECTION

At the peak of my life, as I emerge into my best version, I stand as an entrepreneur, an author, an advocate, a Woman of Faith, and a student of life. Each day is a new dawn to do better. I have learned to see failures and wrong decisions as feedback and to dare to take risks again.

My message to my readers is to join me in this journey of emerging into your best self. On this journey, you will face adversity. How does one stay propelled? By being focused, fearless, and committed to your mission. The journey includes celebrating yourself, forgiving your failures, dreaming again, trying again, and mostly tapping into your full, unique potential. As Marc Nepo says, "We think that accomplishing things will complete us, but it is when we experience life that we will." I am open to experiencing life as it comes.

As I continue climbing the summit of my life and flowing at my unique rhythm, I enjoy every moment while being blissful. I am committed to growing personally and professionally. My prayer to God is to grant me the serenity to accept the things I cannot change, the courage to change the things I can, and the wisdom to know the difference. I am forever grateful to all who have and continue to shape my life.

It starts with investing in yourself. It involves failing repeatedly but never giving up. It requires the courage to pursue your dreams, write that book, start that business, or love again despite past heartbreaks. It's about setting boundaries to protect your inner peace, going to therapy to work through pain, and finding mentors or life coaches to help anchor your ship.

It's about being grateful for those who paved the way and honoring figures like our parents, military, and mentors. It involves serving others—offering your time, being present, actively listening, and providing resources.

As Mel Robbins says, "Your job is to believe it is possible and encourage yourself to keep walking toward it. No matter what, keep believing and give up your timeline for when and how it unfolds."

How Do I Continue to Emerge as My Best Version as an Author?

Evolving into my best version as an author involves various facets. One of the first facets intertwines resilience and persistence in pursuing my dreams. One of my dreams was to become an international bestselling author. This dream kept haunting me, and I could not understand why until I recalled a training session, I attended on the Growth Day platform.

Growth Day

Growth Day is an online platform created by motivator and author Brendon Burchard, among others. I invested in this platform because I am committed to growing personally and professionally. My elder sister, who is also one of my mentors, introduced me to Growth Day. It is a community of diverse individuals who come together to grow and stretch beyond their comfort zones.

The Growth Day platform features speakers, teachers, and coaches from various backgrounds, providing a rich tapestry of knowledge and inspiration. The community offers monthly sessions on topics such as communication, leadership, and more, allowing members to learn from a wide range of experts and perspectives.

Being part of this community has reinforced the importance of resilience and not giving up on my dreams. It has provided me with the tools, support, and inspiration to keep striving towards my goal of becoming an international bestselling author. By surrounding myself with like-minded people and continuously learning, I am constantly growing and evolving in my journey as an author.

I recall a particular teaching by Mel Robbins where she talked about dreams. She explained that dreams don't leave a person; they haunt you until they are fulfilled. Dreams call you forth and activate something deep inside you. This concept resonated deeply with me because one of my lifelong dreams has been to become an author, creating inspiring books that touch hearts and transform lives!

I started writing my first book but stopped for assorted reasons, one being the need to finish graduate school. Balancing school, work, and writing seemed overwhelming, so I decided to postpone my writing and focus on completing my degree. A few years after graduating and starting my career, the dream of writing began to haunt me again.

Determined to take action, I began crafting the art of writing my first book. I was surprised to learn that writing is therapeutic. It is a place to reflect, regenerate, teach, empower, listen, learn, ignite, and grow. Writing brings such peace and liberation. I felt a profound sense of freedom and fulfillment.

Another facet includes courage and learning from my failures. Every failure holds a lesson waiting to be discovered or pondered. Each of us is uniquely created with immense potential, but without unraveling that potential, we deny ourselves, others, and the world a chance at greatness. As Les Brown aptly says, "Everyone has greatness within themselves."

The final facet is service and tenacity. It doesn't matter when or how your purpose is discovered; what matters is how you use it to contribute to others. It's never too early or too late; it's about the impact you make and the legacy you leave. Everything that has transpired in my life, both good and bad, serves a divine purpose. From my internal knowledge, I understand that true success is found through service. It is by serving others and the world that one lives a fulfilling life.

I plan to continue unleashing my full potential and greatness through service. As I evolve, I have transitioned from merely wishing or dreaming to taking decisive action. I am actively crafting my first book and embarking on the road to entrepreneurship. You can do the same!

Embracing these facets—resilience, continuous learning, courage, reflection, supportive communities, service, and tenacity—has allowed me to grow as an author and a person. By integrating these principles into your life, you too can unlock your full potential and contribute to the world in meaningful ways.

ACKNOWLEDGMENT

I want to start by expressing profound gratitude to the Almighty God for guiding and directing this book. I also want to extend special thanks to my mother, Elizabeth, whose inspiration paved the way for me to embark on crafting my first book.

To my beloved father Joseph, and my siblings Beatrice, Jane, and Boniface, your unwavering love and support have been my steadfast pillars. I also want to express immense appreciation to Dr. K. N. Jacob and his wife Mercy for their continual coaching, unwavering mentorship, and thoughtful guidance. I am forever grateful for the impactful imprint you've left on my life.

A sincere thank you to my dear friend Florence for your friendship and inspiration. Special gratitude to my sister Beatrice for setting ambitious standards and providing enduring inspiration.

To my nieces and nephews, I hope that my journey, brimming with both failures and successes, serves as an empowering example.

Thanks to my editor and publisher for their help in organizing and refining this publication, and for bringing the ideas together into a unified narrative. A special thank you to Stephanie for being a beacon of light in my personal and professional life. I am truly grateful to have you on my team.

To my cousins John and Paul, your gracious hospitality upon my relocation to Atlanta, Georgia, and the sagacious wisdom you shared have been invaluable. Special acknowledgment goes to my mentors and role models who have significantly shaped my perspective and contributed profoundly to my growth.

Heartfelt thanks to Dr. Lorna for consistently being a staunch champion in my life. I am grateful to all my friends who have served as unwavering beacons of light. A heartfelt thank you goes to the Women of Faith for their substantial role in my spiritual journey.

As individuals, our journey to tap into our potential mandates stretches beyond our comfort zones. Activists like Rosa Parks, who exhibited courage by refusing to yield her seat, ignited a transformative awakening toward justice. In sharing my journey, I aspire to unveil and explore beyond the confines of my comfort zone. Are you willing to hatch an egg to discover the profound potential lying underneath?

May this book inspire, relate, challenge, and resonate with you, dear reader, as we embark on the transformative path to emerging as our most formidable selves.

ABOUT THE BOOK

This book draws inspiration from the author's strong-willed mother, the Women of Faith, and the brave men and women who have paved the way for many others. It is filled with inspiring stories, life lessons, and her personal journey. As the late Maya Angelou wisely said, "When you learn, teach; when you get, give." Through sharing her life journey, the author hopes to inspire others to hatch their own egg and discover their profound potential.

ABOUT THE AUTHOR

Born in Nairobi, Kenya, the author moved to the United States in pursuit of a better life. She now resides in Atlanta, Georgia. Her journey is a testament to resilience, courage, and the relentless pursuit of dreams.

INSPIRED BY LOVE
MAURINA HOMECARE AGENCY

Maurina Homecare Agency was inspired by my grandparents' journey with dementia, where I witnessed the power of compassion and small acts of kindness in caregiving. Combining my healthcare experience with personal insight, I founded the agency to prioritize empathy and human connection. Our mission is to treat every client with dignity, respect, and genuine care, creating a partnership with families and enriching lives through heartfelt compassion.

Our Services:

- ✓ Personal Care
- ✓ Companion.Sitter
- ✓ Skilled Nursing
- ✓ Dementia and Alzheimers Care

Why Choose Us

- ✓ Exceptional Caregivers & Nurses
- ✓ Customized Care Plans
- ✓ 24/7 Care

" Maurina Homecare Agency has been a blessing for our family. Their caregivers bring kindness, patience, and a sense of joy that truly brighten my mom's days. The peace of mind they've provided is invaluable."

-Jeri Z., whose trust since 2023 inspires us every day.

Contact Us:

- 📞 404 - 973 - 0500
- 🌐 www.maurinahomecare.com
- ✉ iinfo@maurinahomeacare.com

www.ingramcontent.com/pod-product-compliance
Lightning Source LLC
Chambersburg PA
CBHW071714090426
42738CB00009B/1774